YOUR LIFE IN YOUR HANDS

Learn to understand yourself and others with this fascinating and scientific guide to the occult art of palmistry.

With clear illustrations and an easy-to-follow text, YOUR LIFE IN YOUR HANDS explains the meanings of the lines on your palm and the interpretations of the ridge patterns on palm and fingers as well as the shape of the hand itself.

This complete guide can reveal your hidden personality, help you to prepare for your future and to achieve your life's goals.

Your Life In Your Hands

Beryl B. Hutchinson

PAPERBACK LIBRARY, INC.

NEW YORK

PART ONE

*

CHIROGNOMY

CHAPTER I
Chirology

CHAPTER II
Chirognomy

CHAPTER III
Fingers

CHAPTER IV
Thumb

CHAPTER V
Back of the Hand

CHAPTER VI
Gesture

PART TWO

*

DERMATOGLYPHICS

PART THREE

*

CHIROMANCY

PART FOUR

*

CHIROLOGY AND ANATOMY

PART ONE

*

CHIROGNOMY

CHAPTER I

CHIROLOGY

THERE ARE three distinct approaches to hand interpretation which have to be appreciated separately, then woven into a pattern of cause and effect to obtain a true map of the personality.

Chirognomy. The study of Shape. This aspect comprises the thickness and form of palm; the relative length of fingers and thumb and includes the breadth, tip formation, flexibility and shape of the joints; colour and texture of the nails and skin; plus the way the hands are used in gesture.

The observation of shape is the ABC of hand-interpretation, and a never-failing source of interest whether in television talks, newspaper photographs, or in ordinary contact with our fellow men.

The shape of the hand does not usually alter very quickly, but it does alter with changes of occupation which involve a change of outlook. Fingers have become straight after mental training, as quoted by Spier in a classical case of a man of thirty whose first fingers straightened with the success of his psychiatric treatment. Hands often show the failing energies of old age and illness.

A good deal of work on anatomical measurements has been done in France concerning the proportion of hands to height, to the face and relative lengths within the hand itself. This followed the early work in identification by M. Bertillon. The late M. Henri Mangin made French Chirology known to the world, and his study of nails seems to be unique.

The German, Julius Spier, who did so much to win acceptance of the value of hand interpretation by his lectures in Zurich and other centres, taught his pupils to make the most detailed deductions from the back or nail side of upraised hands.

Since the attributes of the various areas of the hand have to be clarified before we can understand the real objective of this book—the underlying meaning of skin pattern—the first approach will be Chirognomy.

Chiromancy, the study of lines, suffers from its history of exile in gypsy encampments. Time will eventually bring acceptance of the value of flexure lines as the indication of our awareness of the areas of energy where they are etched. At present lines arouse sub-conscious tensions, defences, and inherited bogies so that even clear-minded men feel discomfort as they peep into their own hands, yet cannot resist little stories of discovery when writing their books.

Lines change very easily at the bidding of thought and of health. This facility for change will be observed frequently when we examine their paths and their values.

There seems to be a law of Nature that when Man has gone a long way towards perfection in one branch of endeavour a new branch arises to make the seeming perfection obsolete or inadequate. The *Cutty Sark* had to make way for iron ships and steam. The regular mail coaches handed over their commercial value to the railway. In the same way the genius of Cheiro may be seen to mark the culmination of the gypsy tradition, inaugurated by the Frenchmen Desbarolles and d'Arpentigny, indexed by St. Germain and subsequently quoted by every writer on hands.

Now the third approach, first suggested by the Czech Doctor Purkenje in 1823, has taken over the attention of the scientific world.

Dermatoglyphics is the name given to the study of the ridge and furrow patterns on our palms and the soles of our feet (Greek—*Derma*: skin. *Glyphe*: carve).

These patterns are the basis of police identification the world over, while in India and China thumb prints were used as or in addition to the signature to prevent forgery of important documents. Skin patterns are the subject of biological and genetic research in America and at the Galton Laboratory, London University; and the basis of most illuminating psychiatric work in Switzerland and Germany.

Indian tradition sees in the formation of the ridges and furrows the sacred key to man's Karma. While reincarnation is not universally accepted in the West, we can acknowledge that the patterns formed by the papillary ridges and furrows show the basic attitude to life which will colour all the potential as shown by the shape, and the use that is being made of that potential as indicated by the lines.

The actual pattern of the sweat glands and nerve endings which form the ridge and furrow is unchanging though we will see in Part II how they can fall out of line in threatened ill-health, can grow with the hand and shrink again in old age.

The texture will also be found to break down with work involving the use of detergents or acids which harm the skin, but the dots and strokes which remain follow the original pattern which returns with the restoration of health to the skin.

I have been told that even after severe burns necessitating skin graft, when the healing process brings the natural skin to the surface the pattern has reappeared in its original form.

*   *   *

Since no serious study of hands can be made without prints, for recording and for appreciating the minutiae of skin ridges, the procedure is explained in this first chapter, so that the enthusiastic student may find easy reference.

The requirements are:

A roller as used in photographic or lino work. The width should be adequate to ink right across a palm but a smaller size is more convenient for children.

Reeves' finger-print ink, obtainable in small tubes and is far the most convenient to use but, in emergency, the thinner Gestetner printing ink can be used. Being rather thin it is more 'runny' and requires more care. The thicker duplicating inks tend to block the niceties of skin patterns.

A piece of glass or, where glass is not obtainable, any shiny substance such as the inside lid of a biscuit tin, but it must be completely smooth.

Paper. A typing paper without watermark is my own preference but some exponents prefer a more shiny paper. Absence of any watermark within the paper is most desirable.

A small rubber pad which will fill in the hollow part of the palm or a small rolling pin or office ruler.

A pencil or cheap ball-point pen.

A tube of Dirty Paws from Boots or a mixture of surgical spirit and soft soap or any other cleansing agent. *Dirty Paws* has the advantage of being very gentle to the most delicate skin, obtainable in a convenient tube and efficient.

Some cotton wool or cleaning tissue to remove the worst of the ink.

The whole equipment can be obtained for less than £1.

Rough prints can be obtained with watercolour paint or lipstick but these methods are so far from the ideal that they should be kept for the registration of some peculiarity noted when one's own tools are not available.

Procedure

Squeeze about $\frac{1}{4}$ inch of ink on to the glass. With a new roller a little more will be needed and sometimes the ink has to be slightly renewed for the second hand.

Roll the roller until the ink is spread evenly all round. I try on the tip of my own finger to see that I have about the right consistency and to avoid making black blobs on the print. To avoid edge lines on the print run the extreme edge of the roller on a piece of old newspaper so that a thin, dark line is removed from each end.

Starting on the more quiescent hand (left hand of a right-handed person and vice versa), ask that the hand may be held loosely, unclenched, and roll the ink over the palm and up the fingers as evenly as possible.

Have the hand placed upon the paper, begging the owner to put it down naturally and refrain from using the muscles by pressing, gripping, etc.

Outline carefully with the ball-point.

Hold the paper down and have the hand raised clear.

Experience only can tell when a hand print is more accurate with a pad beneath the palm or whether a second print over the roller is essential, but, on the whole, a flexible hand is all right with the pad and a stiff or very high mounted hand is better with the longer procedure.

In any palmar print the thumb will not be adequately

Fig. 1—Thumb on table

shown, so, when the print of the palm is satisfactory, ink the thumb alone. Protecting the table with newspaper, have the fingers placed under the edge so that the whole of the thumb can be printed and outlined on the paper above. Here there is a tendency to press the thumb heavily on the paper but a small jest about a wide thumb showing a resistant will usually gets an accurate picture.

Examine the print with a magnifying glass to be sure that all ridges are clear. If there is any question of the accuracy of finger or thumb pattern the digit may be rolled from one side to the other to show the full extent of the pattern. Do not allow it to be rolled back again or the whole print will be spoiled.

The palmar print will now be seen to stop under the first finger with a blank space to the outline. For any appreciation of childhood problems and of time, this missing part of the hand is essential.

Protecting the table anew, and having inked the edge of

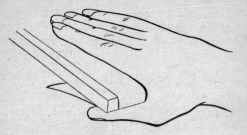

Fig. 2—Thumb under table

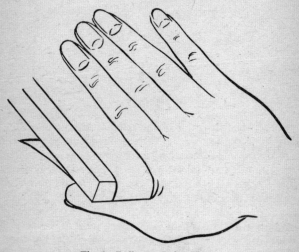

Fig. 3—Roll onto Index Finger

the hand at the side of the first finger where the palmar ridges end, have the hand placed flat upon the paper which has been about one third folded underneath. Have the thumb under the edge and the hand pushed as far onto the table as the

thumb permits. Then, still pressing into the table edge, have
the little finger lead the others turning over inwards as far
as the arm allows. Then remove the hand without going back
to the flat position.

To obtain an accurate position on the main print measure
the distance from the start of Life Line or Head Line to any
two angles which can be identified on the main print and mark
the distance.

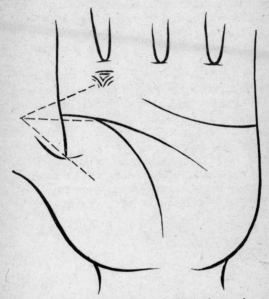

Fig. 4—Measure to tri-radius of Mt. Jupiter and one other point.

Should the main print be inadequate with a hollow centre
(Plain of Mars) the police method must be tried.

Place an edge of paper on the roller as near to the body
as is comfortable. Starting with the second or longest finger
and allowing the others to join in naturally, roll the paper
away from the body. Do *not* force the printing hand but press
it gently as it passes the difficult part, either yourself or with
the owner's other hand.

It is always better to take at least two prints to ensure absolute accuracy.

When one hand is completed wipe off any surplus ink with cotton wool or tissue starting from the tips of the fingers so that the ink cannot get under the nails. When fairly clear leave a piece of the cleaner in the dirty hand as a reminder to keep away from clothes, etc.

When both hands are printed and roughly cleaned follow the directions on whatever cleansing medium is used but wash off in *cold* water. This is an old engineering trick which does stop any dirt getting into the pores of the skin. When the ink is safely removed the hands may be washed in warm water in the usual way.

Prints should be dated immediately and identified either by filing system number or by name if the owner does not object. Notes should also be made from the backs of the hands:

a. Colour of skin and texture.
b. Nails.
c. Knots and flexibility.
d. Any peculiarities including any injuries or anything affecting the immediate condition of the hands.

Careful records over the years are fascinating, and can be so helpful when difficulties have to be overcome.

CHAPTER II

CHIROGNOMY

CHIROLOGISTS regard the hand as a map, each area having its own association with some aspect of the individuality. The art of good interpretation lies in the accurate assessment of the strength or weakness of each ingredient and the balance between them. For example, is control strong enough to guide impetuous enthusiasm?

The strength of an area is judged by its relative size, development and dominance in relation to the rest of the hand.

The divisions used can be closely correlated with anatomy, so the more striking relationships will be mentioned in the survey of the palm, while more detailed anatomy may be studied in Part IV.

Transverse Division

Three main divisions are recognized across the palm between the wrist and the base of the fingers. The symbol I have found most effective for my pupils is illustrated by the picture of a tree (Fig. 5). From its roots a tree draws life. The hand shows the capacity for life by the size and consistency of the lowest third—from the wrist to a parallel line starting from where the thumb joins the palm under the first finger.

The ball of the thumb is known to anatomists as the Thenar Eminence and to chirologists as the Mount of Venus. The area on the opposite, or percussion, side is the Hypothenar Eminence or Mount of Luna. Between Venus and Luna above the centre of the wrist is sometimes found a Mount of Neptune.

It is not present on all hands and has no special anatomical name.

The Middle Area extends to the upper transverse line (Line of Heart) under the second, third and fourth fingers, but continues straight across under the first finger, using as its boundary there the beginning of the Line of Life which lies around the thumb.

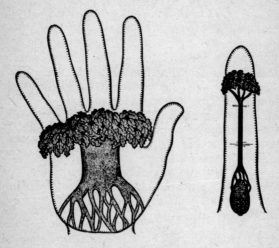

Fig. 5—A tree as a symbol: palm   Fig. 6—A tree as a symbol: finger

The whole of the middle section takes the name of the God of Energy, Mars. Of course the darker side of the God was his quarrelsomeness, but even that may be perverted energy—a lazy person rarely quarrels.

The area of conscious energy, closely united with physical courage, is found just above the thumb in line with the first finger. The outer or percussion side shows the degree of development of instinctive courage or fortitude. The tree symbol is especially suitable here, with the energies flowing up the outer circumference of the trunk immediately under the bark, while the part that the world uses, the central wood of the tree, has its counterpart in the middle of the hand. This central area relates to courage in social contacts and our ability to make a living. For example, a person may have the courage of the proverbial lion yet not be able to see through the blandishments of a colleague or, having seen, resist.

As a tree culminates in leaf, flower and fruit, so Man's highest expression is in his power of thought. The uppermost third of the palm between the upper transverse line and the base of the fingers is the area of mental interests, the foundation for the repetition of a renewed tree pattern in the fingers.

Longitudinal Divisions

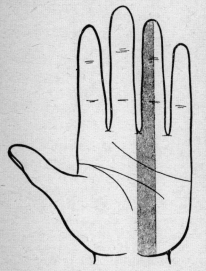

The hand is also divided longitudinally with imaginary boundaries from fingers to wrist. These areas follow the paths of the Radial, Median and Ulna nerves, so the middle one is not exact, as it represents overlap between the conscious and instinctive, even as the nerves stray into each other's territory.

The first two fingers, half the third finger, the area of the palm beneath and part of the thumb are served by the Median nerve. This part of the hand is

Fig. 7—Longitudinal divisions

related to the Conscious Self, while the percussion or outer side of the hand, with the little finger and the other half of the third finger, the area of the Ulna nerve, expresses the submerged or Instinctive Self and its response to the outside world.

Boundaries

Direction and measurement often require a name for the identification of the boundary of the palm. The actual line is where the pattern of ridge and furrow merges into the more random covering of normal skin. A very fine texture may need a magnifying glass to distinguish the division with certainty.

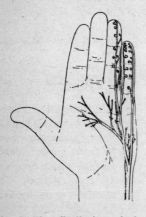

Fig. 8—The distribution of the ulna nerve in the palm of the hand. The nerves beset with Pacinian bodies are sensory branches. The shaded branches are motor. (Wood Jones: *The Principles of Anatomy as seen in the Hand*, Baillière, Tindall & Cassell.)

Fig. 9—The distribution of the median nerve in the palm of the hand. The nerves beset with Pacinian bodies are sensory branches. The shaded branches are motor. (Wood Jones: *The Principles of Anatomy as seen in the Hand*, Baillière, Tindall & Cassell.)

The *Ulna* nerve gives its name to the outer or percussion edge of the hand. Opposite, where the thumb shares branches from the *Radial* nerve, that name is used for the boundary. *Proximal* is obviously next to the wrist, with the line of the fingers as *Distal*. In English we can speak of a thumb and four fingers or of five digits, with the Index acting as both first finger and second digit, so it is equally correct to speak of the line at the base of the fingers as *Digital*.

ANALYSIS OF PALM

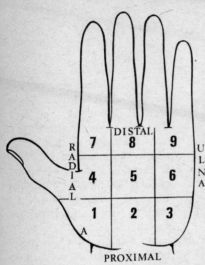

Fig. 10—Diagrammatic areas of palm and boundaries. a). Angle of sound.

To become thoroughly accustomed to these divisions and areas, let us return to the lowest third (1, 2, 3 in Fig. 10) starting with the Mount of Venus. This base of the thumb expresses the physical aspect of 'I live', which includes the capacity to enjoy being alive. The mount should be firm yet springy, padded well out towards the centre of the hand, yet allowing the whole division to be in proportion to the rest of the palm. The big main blood vessels form their arches and branches under the safety afforded by thumb muscles, so the better the blood vessels the more life there can be in the hand. Hobbies such as fencing, involving the use of the thumb, can increase the size of this mount but such pursuits can also increase life energy. The owner would not have taken up these forms of work and exercise had there not been a predisposition towards them. Also the resilience of such muscles warns whether or not they are much employed or are flabbily lustful. A well-made mount indicates a capacity to live, but that includes the capacity for warmth of emotion, of enthusiasm, and of appreciation of the emotional arts, especially music.

When a hand is held out there is often an angle formed at the lower, wrist edge of the ball of the thumb. Should this angle be pronounced it shows an appreciation of the vibration of sound. Usually, in, say, eighty-five per cent of hands, this angle may be interpreted as an appreciation of music, but the appreciation may be the recognition of aircraft or joy in the hum of a ship's engine (Fig. 10a).

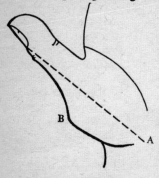

Fig. 11—a). To test true pitch
b). Angle of time

There is a definite law governing our judgement of mounts. The higher the mount, the better the *quality*. The larger the mount, the greater the *quantity* of its attribute. Place a pencil or edge of a piece of paper on an outstretched hand from the corner of the thumb-nail to the mount of Neptune. If there is a ridge of higher padding creating a watershed effect, it will indicate 'true pitch', a very accurate ear for sound.

A distinct angle where the thumb actually leaves the palm indicates order in Time. This order may take the form of an appreciation of rhythm should the lower angle suggest any love of music; or the order in Time may take the form of instinctive punctuality. When someone strolls up to a train, arranges the hand luggage and sits back exactly as the guard blows the whistle, one may be sure of a pronounced example of the angle of order in Time. When watching television this angle can be noted on the hands of the more subtle comedians.

On the opposite, percussion, side of the hand lies the Mount of Luna. Starting from the wrist this mount embodies racial memories, merging into ancestral, then childhood experiences until, where it becomes one with the area of Mars Negative, it appears to keep the stored memory of everything we have experienced and learned. Imagination may be drawn from all these things and twist them so that their origins are obscured, but we cannot imagine anything without some starting point of memory as a foundation.

The basis for this interpretation of Luna comes from the observation of how it is manifested. When the mount appears to drop into the wrist it shows an at-one-ness with Nature's rhythms and cycles. No dancer is ever without this well-formed corner of the Luna mount; but it is not always used for dancing. One may meet with it on the hands of a 'green-fingered' specialist in plant grafting or, with a strong mount above, an ornithologist. A good, strong, hard mount is found on the hands of farmers and navigators, showing their feeling for the weather. Sometimes the padding is very high, even pink tinged, when the height shows a quality of perception which the colouring increases to psychic sensitivity. A person with such a mount will be acutely aware of 'atmosphere' among people, in buildings, or in dowsing. The make-up of Edwardian ladies included the delicate colouring of the percussion, partly to narrow the look of the palm and partly to indicate their sensitivity.

As the mount merges almost imperceptibly into Mars Negative, more modern memories and impressions are stored until, about half-way up a normal palm, there is a fully active supra-conscious response to things learned. The importance of this area will be appreciated later when studying the lines of the hand.

Mount of Neptune

This mount does not have true boundaries. It is just a filling up of the centre of the palm next to the wrist as opposed to the hand with a distinct hollow between Venus and Luna. The effect when present is strong. The Life Force seems to flow so freely through the owner that a magnetism is given out. Such formation is found on the hands of doctors, nurses and less orthodox healers; all who make people feel better when they enter the room. No public speaker can get across the foot-lights without this bar across the base of the hand, but when it is very pronounced a speaker can give pleasure by reciting the ABC.

The Mount of Neptune may well prove to have a relation-ship with the pineal gland in that gland's physical manifesta-tion, and may gauge the cosmic radiation boosting the life energy shown by the base mounts. However, that is an eso-teric thought and cannot yet be supported factually.

There is an atavistic blood vessel, which used to enter a hand in the centre and is sometimes present even yet, that also may prove to have some connection with a good Mount of Neptune and the extra vitality which it indicates.

Area of Mars (Fig. 10, 4)

The positive aspect of physical courage is sought alongside and just above the thumb, but within the Life Line. When the hand is clenched a little wodge of flesh sometimes shows at the back of the hand, forced up by the tightening of the thumb. This is known as 'the mouse' and shows that the instinct of physical courage is strong. On the palm a poor area looking as though it was formed by just webbing does not constitute a coward; but it does mean that any physical courage shown will be the result of character and not a natural instinct.

Opposite to this mount, usually between the two transverse lines but always beneath the upper one, is the Mount of Mars Negative (Fig 10, 6). When well developed and firm it demonstrates that persistence in the face of adversity which we recognize as Fortitude. Some authorities seek moral courage in this area; the instinct to hang on when the odds are against one is very necessary to a display of moral courage. This development is often seen on the hands of men who endure great hardship, and it may be found with quite a poor Positive Mars, in which case it compensates for the lack of the reckless variety of courage.

I have not seen very many Russian hands, but in those I have seen, both in fact and in photographs, a very high development of this mount of Mars Negative appears to be present. It may be the result of the Russian climate, but possibly an aspect of the national character worthy of consideration when dealing with these people.

Between the mounts, across the middle of the hand, is found the Plain of Mars (Fig 10, 5). Since the main lines of the hand traverse the area it obviously has great importance in any assessment of personality, but careful judgement must be exercised as the appearance can be deceptive. When the surrounding mounts are very well developed the Plain can look poor and thin. Here one must feel with a thumb on the palm and fingers on the back of the hand. When the bones seem uncovered, with no substance between one's finger and thumb, the centre of the palm is weak. If it feels hard and substantial then the Plain is strong and any appearance of hollowness comes from the height of the surrounding mounts.

There are many traditions and sayings about a hollow palm (one name is 'the beggar's bowl'), but the basic meaning may be taken as showing a lack of energy in worldly affairs. Since the important lines affecting the career pass over this area, feebleness there suggests a feebleness about worldly relations. There seems a close connection too with an incapacity for selecting friends and advisers. People are thrown together and become friendly by propinquity, even though they would not become friends were they not working or playing under the same conditions. A strong, firm hand will assess the value of that friendship and not allow it to intrude on judgement. The feeble Plain will know the connection is not wise, nor even pleasant, but will not shake it off and, worse, may allow itself to be influenced by the so-called friend. This is a common weakness in young hands, where the right word of warning often helps to balance over-enthusiastic school friendships.

The top part of the palm is partly owned by the fingers. Hold the hand straight up, thumb towards you, then bend the fingers to a right angle.

It will be seen that the finger mounts cover the joint. It is as though that mental area of the palm is the soil out of which the fingers grow (Fig. 12).

When the little pads are high and elastic they will give life to the capacity for interest and instinctive thought. People with such pads never grow old in mind. When the hand is flat and even bony-looking beneath the fingers thinking may be painstaking, exact, brilliant in analysis or laboratory work, but ideas tend to become dry and routine ridden.

These eminences cannot be placed under the second or third fingers, or indeed directly under the fourth. See Fig. 13. This explains that tendons lie across this area on their way to the fingers, while the pads protect the marshalling yard of nerves and blood vessels as they organize themselves for their safe journey up the sides of each finger.

In old books one reads much about 'displaced' mounts when learning about these protective pads of fascia. The correct placing of a finger mount is found in the skin pattern only and any other suggestion is ignorant nonsense.

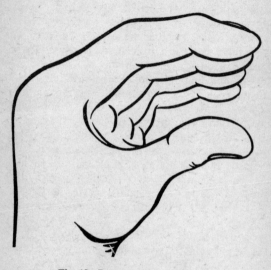

Fig. 12—Between palm and fingers

The first finger has its own muscular arrangement and can have a bulge towards the edge of the hand, as can the little finger, but any fullness will show on the edge of the hand and a line will often suggest the tendon beneath the centre of the finger.

Mrs. St. Hill saw the mount under Jupiter finger as a sign of pride, the proximity to finger or heart line showing the type of pride. I have not been able to follow her completely, but I have found that a pronounced mount placed towards the centre of the hand goes with pride in family or regiment or any tribal type group to which the owner belongs.

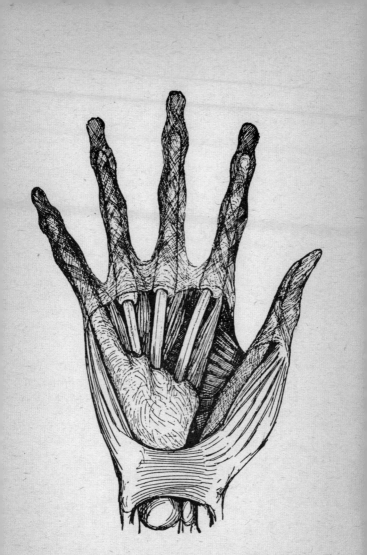

Fig. 13—The palmar bursa and the sheaths of the flexor tendons. The anterior annular ligament is left in position. (Wood Jones. *The Principles of Anatomy as seen in the Hand*, Baillière, Tindall & Cassell.)

The centre of the three mounts seems to give vitality to the interest in one's occupation, while the third, between third and fourth fingers, aids wit and social relationship. However, I am not completely happy about their individual meanings and prefer to take them together as stated.

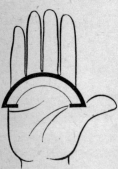

The digital boundary of the palm will be found of great importance when studying the true value of the fingers. Just as no plant can maintain growth out of poor or unsuitable soil, so the best, most shapely finger will lack confidence in itself if the palm beneath does not support it.

I liken the line of the boundary to an architectural arch. The normal, middle way is like a Norman arch with the keystone at the Medius finger. Strong, balanced, this form supports the fingers without either diffidence or aggressiveness.

Fig. 14—Norman arch

When the two outside fingers are set low as in the Perpendicular arch, there is an obvious lack of support for the two digits which represent the Self in one's mind. There is a clear blue-print of Adler's inferiority complex when the first finger falls away. A self-depreciation, diffidence, unsureness, when the palm tails off under the fourth finger. This will be further considered with the individual fingers.

Fig. 15—Perpendicular arch

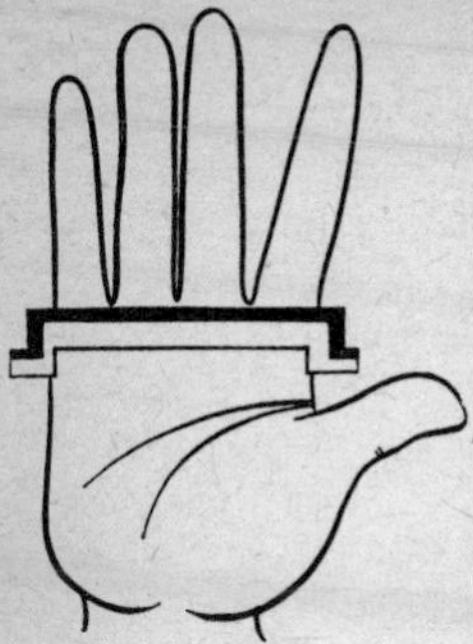

The Tudor arch forms such a strong, equal basis for all the fingers that, to return to our first metaphor, they 'run to wood'. The owners are so full of self-confidence in their hearts that they trust their own judgement right or wrong. In an employment demanding assurance, aggression, push, lies their greatest happiness.

Fig. 16—Tudor arch

The Whole

Now that we have some idea of the meanings of the hand, let us look at the whole. This is working backwards because in practice the whole is assessed for type first of all; but if there is no knowledge of the three worlds and what one is looking at, one cannot appreciate the common sense of the statements about the whole.

Square

Does the palm look square, with the boundary from first finger through the thumb approximately parallel with the boundary from little finger, edging Mars Negative and Luna to the wrist? Is the width across under the fingers about the same measurement as little finger to wrist? If so, the palm is square and well balanced, practical with good adjustment between physical and mental aspects. Little square palms are often found on women's hands, especially on the Continent where good housekeeping is a natural instinct. Their fingers may have other interests, but the little square palms will make light of such tasks. They give equal balance to men's hands, but one expects to find them on reliable husbands, brothers and advisers.

Often there is a pronounced curve to the percussion side of the hand which is known as the 'creative' curve. I prefer to think of it as the curve of energy, as it follows the rules of the three worlds. Low down level with the Luna mount, it tells of physical energy; higher, towards Mars, the energy is shown as persistence in the face of difficulties, an energizing of the fortitude of Mars. Logically the two names have the same meaning when the curve is midway, because energy and drive are essential to make dreams come to reality; there is a great

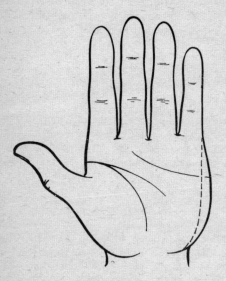

Fig. 17—Creative curve

deal of hard work behind creation in any milieu, with the higher the visualization the harder the work.

When a hand is otherwise square with only a sort of bow-window of a curve, it keeps its balanced practical aspect, only adding the attribute of energy to carry out its designs, but when the whole palm is wider than the length from Medius finger base to wrist, the accent is on a more restless type of energy. Such people must have an open air life. If they are restricted in their work they must be able to get out into the air directly

the day's work is done and if at all possible they must not
be confined to an office. The ideal occupation, apart from the
obvious open air hard work, must enable them to use their
vigour in a constructive way.

When the curve to the percussion is high, immediately under
the little finger, the energy will be purely mental. This is
virtually a widening of the mount under the little finger, but
with no corresponding strength in the lower part of the hand
it indicates people who live on their nerves and who will go
on working long after they should rest, though with a short
rest they can usually recover quickly. This widening beneath
the fingers is called 'Spatulate' hand, one in which the wrist
is narrow and the whole hand widens at the top of the palm.

Conic

The opposite of the Spatulate palm is the Conic. Here the
base of the hand is wide with the finger breadth narrow. As
we have seen from the reading of the mounts, the sphere of
energy will be in the physical world. This formation needs
especial care and must be considered with other factors such
as the tips of the digits, skin pattern, skin texture and lines,
as the interpretation may vary from the sensual dreams of a
soft-skinned, pointed-fingered voluptuary to the hard, lean
hands of a rather mentally or traditionally restricted sporting
type, so the balance demands a high degree of discretion.

Long Palms

A rectangular palm is frequently found among city dwellers.
At first glance the parallel sides may appear square, but then
it is realized that the measurement would be considerably
longer from wrist to finger base than the width across, and that
the effect is not due to a lack of a curve of energy.

In the rectangular palm the balance is good between physical, emotional and mental planes, but there will be a preference
for indoor work and hobbies. Very often when the hand is
thin through or lacking in substance, the owner will drive
himself to do the things he feels he should, in which case the
palm will be heavily lined to show that such pursuits are being
followed by the expenditure of nervous energy and not from

an instinctive feeling for an arduous life. The quality of perception may be high, and the type is invaluable in a largely urban world. High mounts on a long, narrow hand are difficult to assess correctly from prints only and, when encountered, the warning about taking several prints should be remembered.

A long, delicate palm with fingers to match used to be considered a great beauty and was assigned to many aristocratic portraits, as may be seen in picture galleries. Are such hand studies compliments, truth, or the only shape the artist could draw?

CHAPTER III

FINGERS

FINGERS PORTRAY our spheres of interest or instinctive thought. They follow the same symbol of the tree in that the section or phalange nearest the palm depicts our interest in physical things, the middle section corresponds to our lower mental or common sense, while the nail phalange shows our capacity for thought both abstract and pictured. The nail phalange is numbered first, the middle one second and the base is spoken of as the third.

The respective lengths of the section should be measured to get a true analysis. When measuring look at the side of the finger, as a joint may show several lines across, but only one will continue around to the side, and that may be taken as the true length of a phalange.

Fingers will supply other data from their length, straightness, crookedness or wilting, the natural angle of opening, the way they are set on the palm and the shape of the tips.

We will take a general study of the information first and then apply the knowledge to each finger in turn.

Length

When fingers look short in relation to the palm the thought process will be quick. Short-fingered people like large headings in print, clear paragraphs and 'over-all' schemes; in sum they like to see the Whole.

People with long fingers enjoy the process of thinking and they like detailed and exact thought. When a short-fingered person has to work on detail he goes for it rather like a terrier

at a rat hole—the data has to be got out, the calculation made
before he can rest, but he is much happier if he can find a
long-fingered person to prepare the particulars ready for him.

The question of what is actually meant by long and short
fingers beyond just looking at the obvious ones, is rather
difficult.

For true measurement the middle finger is taken on the
back of the hand from knuckle to tip and compared with the
length of the palm from that finger to wrist. Such measurements I have not found sufficiently differentiated to be satisfactory and, after many years of experiment, I have decided
that the actual bone lengths are not the basis of the apparent
divergence with the palm. The true link is between large im-
pinging mounts taking up a great deal of the finger bones,
showing the ascendency of palmar energy, thus causing apparent shortness of the fingers. This dominance of the palm would
explain the quick, decisive impatience which undoubtedly
follows a second finger which measures on the palmar side
less than seven-eighths of the whole palm yet is in balance
with its companion first and third fingers.

French exponents have devoted much attention to relative
measurements, yet have found but small differences in the
finger-palm ratio, though there is a large variation between
the size of a person and his hands. Both the French and
Chinese expect the third or basal phalange to be longer than
the other two. This tendency may well be related to the
instinctive love of the land which one finds even among the
most sophisticated French city dwellers, while the Chinese
are world-famed for their knowledge and skill in horticulture.

Straightness

Fingers should be straight as though standing proudly on
their own bases. They often lean gently or wilt towards each
other as though drawn by the superior strength of an adjoin-
ing interest. They can also be definitely crooked, but before
telling a client that such and such untoward aspects are shown,
it is as well to compare the two hands and make certain that
the kink is not the result of an accident. Sometimes one is
told that knobs and twists are the result of rheumatism, which

may be fully appreciated, but why did the rheumatism lodge in that particular joint? There are so many types of that tiresome complaint that one cannot be dogmatic, but there is a field of interest in seeing how often the acid deposits follow chirological tradition.

Tips

Dr. Benham, the eminent American chirologist, illustrates the value of the different shape of tip very graphically by

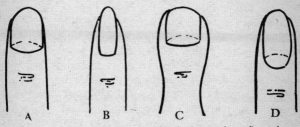

Fig. 18—Tips: a). square; b). pointed; c). spatulate; d). conic

saying that the hand is a terminal for the Life Force as it enters the body from the outside air. He mentions that when a baby draws its first breath it stretches out its hands to begin its life. I have no experience with babies, but I have often watched poodle puppies stretching out their front paws before the first life-announcing sneeze.

Palmists recognize seven types of finger tips but four classifications are quite enough for general use—pointed, conic, square and spatulate (Fig. 18).

Dr. Benham visualizes Life Force flowing in at the tips of square-shaped fingers carefully, systematically, into each corner before going on its way, giving judgement of eye, accuracy of reception and thought, a balance and often an inherent sense of justice to instinctive thoughts before sending them on to the brain.

Through pointed tips (Fig. 18, B) the Life Force flows swiftly, carrying ideas so directly that they appear to be intuitive or inspired. Pointed fingers excel in ideas and talk, but sustained action follows only if the thumb is strong and rules them.

The opposite extreme is called 'Spatulate' (Fig. 18, C). It shows a little bulge each side of the nail. The type is decided from the appearance of the flesh and has nothing to do with the nail itself. When there is any doubt as to whether a tip is square or spatulate, a piece of white paper held alongside the finger will help the eye to see and decide which shape predominates. Imagine that to create the bulge the entering ideas have swirled round in the finger tips before starting their journey to the brain, making the fingers themselves alive with the ideas they have assimilated. Spatulate finger tips are a sure sign of people who like to do things with their hands. A schoolmistress Fellow of the S.S.P.P. reports that small boys frequently have this type of tip to several of their digits, and when they do they tend to fidget unless they have some means of expressing themselves through their hands. They often want to join one of the Services, hoping to see the world. Girls with spatulate tips are 'tomboys'.

Many English hands have 'Conic' tips (Fig. 18, D), a formation midway between pointed and square. These combine the reception of ideas shown by the pointed fingers with the steadiness and control of the clear-minded square type. The ratio between these two extremes will be shown as a picture in each individual finger tip.

Fig. 19—Droplet

Little pointed bulges on the finger pads are known as 'droplets' (Fig. 19) and indicate a highly developed sense of touch. They are associated primarily with instrumental musicians, but when not needed on musical instruments they test the texture of cloth or wood, or use the sensitivity on the value of antiques. It is said that fingers with these pads rarely drop or break anything.

Flexibility

Or bending back at the joints, is better seen from the back

of the hand. It is the reflection of a flexible mind. For example, should the joint between the nail and middle phalange be able to bend back there will be an intuitional acceptance of ideas; they are accepted for consideration.

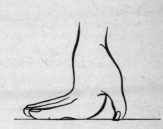

Fig. 20—Flexibility at first and second joints

Fig. 21—Flexibility at knuckles

Flexibility of the second joint between the middle and base sections allows play between common sense and reality, while the ability to bend back at the knuckles, allowing flexibility in material things, will enable a woman to make a home wherever she may find herself or a man to adapt himself to any circumstances demanded by his job.

Knotted Joints

One purpose in tracing round the outline of the hand and fingers when taking a print is to reveal whether the joints have a decided thickening or are smooth. Any thickening portrays an impediment or sieve between the spheres of interest of the phalanges, or it may be seen as a pause for consideration. The enlargement of the first joints between first and second phalanges are known as 'Knots of Philosophy' and arrest the acceptance of ideas without due deliberation. Be careful at this joint to make sure that the swelling is at the joint and not above it between joint and nail. If there is a true knot it can be felt as the top of the digit is moved; but should the joint feel smooth, with the enlargement above, the effect is to give the middle phalange a spatulate top. The interests displayed by the practical-mental sphere will be in doing, in working with the hands.

Knot of Order

Since the second joint unites the world of practical thought with the physical and material, people with these joints knotted have orderly minds and put every idea into its proper place before accepting it. These fingers may not be tidy outwardly, but they will never 'tidy' things into wrong places. They will classify ideas too and will love a system of filing or card indexing, though they may not be able to carry it out for themselves. Their attitude is often incomprehensible to people they live or work with, because they can be the most untidy people possible, yet they are really worried when china is not returned to its correct place or a paper is wrongly filed.

Knuckles

There is no possibility of assessing knuckles from a print, so they will be considered with the back of the hand. STIFF fingers, inbending, show a stiff mind and their inbending proclivities show how tensely they try to have and to hold. This will be discussed further with Gesture.

INDIVIDUAL FINGERS

First Finger

The first or Index finger is an essentially human development; no other animal has this form. It stands for our awareness of Self in a world of other people. Notice how a baby uses the first finger to trace its mother's face and generally to educate its eyes to focus. Jupiter was Lord of the Visible World and one constantly sees how, when this finger is strong and dominant, the Jovian qualities are shown.

The normal length of the Index finger is level with the third and both should attain at least the base of the nail of the second finger, while the ideal proportion is about half-way up the nail when the hand is open, palm upwards. The turn of wrist bones has a deceptive effect on the length of this first finger, as may be observed in a mirror when the hand is turned back and forth, or looked at from the back, held upright, and then placed palm up on a table. This allowance should be remembered when looking at photographs of hands as in a newspaper. Some wrists seem to have more influence than others, but I have not yet found any formula by which one can identify them. When one has a living hand or print and there is any doubt, one should measure with a pencil or stiff paper such as the edge of an envelope. Sometimes the Index finger may be shorter because of the undue length of the third finger, but if it is straight and strong it will retain its meaning of a dominant influence.

When the total length of the Jupiter finger is longer than the third, by however small a margin, a person is indicated who will always find himself in a position of authority. Such hands naturally gravitate to Committees, to responsibility, and are found on the hands of many school and university teachers. Perhaps this shows even more on women's than men's hands, because up till now a stronger effort has to be made by women to attain such posts. Another position often filled by people with dominant first fingers is President of local associations. I would stress that in many cases they do not seek such promotion, but they just seem to be the obvious people to elect for the job. Such positions may also come to straight, strong but shorter fingers.

When Jupiter is well shaped and strong the owner will have a sense of his own position, but the value may vary from an undue sense of his own importance, through ambition, to a sense of responsibility and leadership.

A poor, short, weak first finger is the sign of Dr. Adler's 'Inferiority Complex'. The same effect is apparent when quite a good finger is set too low on the perpendicular arch. In this latter case the owner has to be encouraged to take the position he should and this may lead to a feeling of frustration; he knows he should make something of his life, but cannot start himself on his path.

When the Jupiter finger rises from a very high mount, while the fourth finger is ultra-low, there may be a tiresome 'bossiness'. Compensation is being attempted so that if, far from snubbing this tendency, one praises and reassures, the dominance will fade out as the subject feels less need to boost himself against his inherent self-mistrust.

Jupiter Having decided the total length the question arises as to which is the dominant 'world', and the three phalanges are studied for relative length. The base section demonstrates the appreciation of the sense of taste. A large, fleshy base demands quantity in its meals, whereas a high, slightly pointed padding suggests an accurate sense of taste and is found well expressed on the hands of gourmets and wine and tea tasters. Should this phalange be the longest a career should be sought in catering or some life where the personality can be expressed in physical terms. There can also be a narrowness where the finger joins the palm, with fullness above, just below the next joint. This formation will be found where the owner is quite happy with camping or safari conditions but is hyper-critical when conditions permit. Such hands will do without comforts quite happily, but appreciate the best and have no use for the mediocre.

Should the middle section be long or specially strong there will be an aptitude for craftsmanship, for practical improvements or domestic work. This is especially marked should there be the spatulate effect for this phalange as described. When short, with the other phalanges long, work will be delegated to other people if possible, but if not possible, intelligence will come to the aid of action to concentrate or minimize the work as much as possible.

The nail phalange, when long and developed, is said to typify the priest. That a successful dignitary of the Church has a long first phalanged index finger is quite correct, but any other person filling a position of dignity can have one as well. Education demands a share, in fact any career in which the leadership includes *personal* contact with other people. The wearing of a ring on this finger advertises a focus of this feeling of Self.

A first finger should be straight to attain its full value; one should stand on one's own feet. Leaning towards the straight second finger, it will show a preoccupation with background or home and this is often found on the hands of housewives and mothers. They do not assert themselves for their own satisfaction but from a matriarchal angle of clean necks and dry socks. I have met this wilt of the first finger where men have been responsible for machines as foremen or setting up intricate instruments.

A first finger rarely wilts outwards, but the whole finger may he held apart from the hand meaning 'I myself am independent of background and enjoy independence of thought', or shortly, 'my conscious self is independent of the world.'

Tips

First fingers tend to have conic or pointed tips even when the other digits have spatulate or square. The more pointed the better will the owner be able to grasp the subject matter of a book or deed. This seems to refer mainly to reading and is not as pronounced with hearing, which is more the business of the little finger. However, that is not a rule but just a tendency. Combined with even a slight degree of flexibility at the first joint, the conic or pointedness allows a better knowledge of how and when to contact other people, when to ask a favour, or when to disappear discreetly. The *square tip* is always one of a set when justice, exact and careful assessment of problems will rule. This pattern may follow the legal profession and makes for excellent trustees, bankers or counsellors.

Spatulate tips to first fingers are also rarely found except as one of a set. People with such fingers make worthy citizens, but one is tempted to wish they would sit down and cease to fuss. Nerves can make people over-conscientious and unable to relax but—it may be prejudice—first fingers spatulate seem to do it from pure love of bustle.

Knots at the nail joints betoken a hesitation in accepting other people, leading to scepticism. Never tell a lie to someone with a knotted first finger joint for it just will not be believed. A knotted second joint alone is rare, except as the result of injury, but the love of order will be shown in personal things, in matching clothes and in being careful to return anything borrowed to the exact place whence it came.

Second Finger

The second, Medius, finger of Saturn is the fulcrum of the hand. It is more firmly attached to the wrist bones than any of the others and has fewer muscles to move it sideways. This middle digit of the hand stands for ourselves in relation to our backgrounds, to our property, career and responsibility. I like to picture aboriginal man in his cave, hunting for his mate and family and claiming a bit of ground outside his home to start agriculture. Everything that can possibly be related to that primordial picture is represented by the finger of Saturn. Think of Saturn as the controller and provider.

Over-long in proportion to its comrades, this finger stresses the feeling far too much and may become solitary and unsocial by its narrowness and aloofness. It can show a dedication to science or research in some form, but as the planet Saturn is associated with lead, so an over-developed finger can surround itself with an aura of leadenness.

But, just as lead is necessary to conduct electricity safely, so some Saturnian influence is needed for human conduct. An over-short Medius in relation to the others will show a Bohemian type of mind. This form is often seen on the hands of artists and it is astonishing how many short second fingers are to be seen among people living in the South of France who are not French by birth. The formation is not infrequent among newspaper reporters.

Having decided the total length of the finger, the dominant phalange must be sought. Should the base be longest there will be a special feeling for the land. Gardeners, farmers and woodmen have this phalange longer than the others, and when one sees it on the hands of a young person one has to suggest a career with thoughts of Mother Earth. Miners are also said to have this long base, but I have no prints as proof.

The padding follows the rules. If it is wide, even heavy in appearance, *quantity* will be of primary importance. For example, a farmer with this type of phalange will want a large herd with a heavy milk yield. A high, pointed padding demands excellence or nothing, so this farmer will demand a herd of carefully selected pedigree cows giving milk with a high butter fat content and preferably winning some prizes at shows.

Affinity with Mother Earth should be supported by the Mount of Luna, thus correlating the gift and power of the palm with the instinctive sphere of interest in the mind.

The middle phalange is in accord with growth; all the young life about the cave, whether animal or vegetable, is of interest to a long section. Some practitioners see a confirmation of organizing ability. Certainly when in harmony with the Index finger it ensures a successful housewife who makes her cakes, bottles her fruit and runs the family with efficient skill. One can see these formations, with their little spatulate thickening above the joint, one after another in food shops and Women's Institute gatherings.

A short section lacks this advantage and has to seek the aid of a Mrs. Beeton to achieve results by intelligent theory. If a man, showing no signs of psychopathic nerves, demands that the children be kept quiet while he reads, his middle section will be short and the nail section long.

The nail phalange reflects the intellectual aspect, so that the interest is in the ethical side of religion. Science or any other vocation may be raised to a religion, and the strength of all theories about background affairs, may be judged by the length of the first section. When the two wholly Conscious-Self nail phalanges are longer on the Index and Medius fingers, abstract and pictured thought is paramount. The danger lies in their signifying an intellectual snob, the most trying variety of snobbishness, though some pride in intellect is almost unavoidable that the gift may be respected and used.

We shall find the influence of this first phalange showing in many ways as we look at it during the interpretation of skin patterns and lines.

As with all fingers, Saturn is best when worn straight. Less than one per cent wilt towards Jupiter. Leaning towards the third is, on the contrary, quite frequently found. Here the serious background finger turns to the finger of happiness as a flower to light; the salary side of work is put aside for the job that appeals.

Tips can favour any of the shapes. The square is frequent and finds its fullest expression on the Medius finger because

it allows an instinctive judgement of values, especially in property. The square helps in the grasping of the niceties of legal
documents or a grasp of the small print in hire purchase or
insurance policies. When the finger is rather short the advice
of a man with a square tipped second finger will bear serious
consideration, though he may not act on his own advice.

Spatulate tips are not rare, but usually in companionship
with a spatulate third finger. Active intelligence in mundane
affairs should lead to invention, engineering, architecture or
construction, in fact any career where brain and hand can
work together to express the personality.

Conic tips have their place on Saturn fingers too, but as
one of a set or at least in agreement with the first finger. The
more pointed the tip the less chance there is of instinctive
judgement. People with pointed or conic tips are wise to think
slowly or take expert advice before signing any document.
They have the compensation of intuitive gifts when the joints
are smooth, which increase should the joint be flexible as well.

Flexibility. When the Medius finger is flexible at the upper
nail section joint, there is a gift of intuitive powers which can
be raised to psychic extension of the senses of seeing and
hearing. Mediums who say 'I see', or 'I hear', always have this
type of second finger joint, but when they use 'I feel', they may
acquire their knowledge through a high pink mount of Luna. It
may interest students of occult subjects to know that on the
physical map of the hand the Pineal Gland—seat of the Head
Chakram and the pinpoint connection for positive medium-
ship—is identified with this joint and the tip of this finger.

Flexibility at the second joint between common sense and
the physical world is NOT desirable. This formation allows the
owner to be far too suggestible. He can convince himself of
anything. A famous 'psychic investigator' had a habit of resting
the tips of his fingers on the table while he lectured, showing
the very pronounced bendiness of this joint. Whichever way
he began to talk, whether with belief or scepticism, by the
end he had convinced himself of the opposite interpretation.

Third Finger

The third, ring finger, is usually associated with Art and

is named for Apollo, charioteer of the Sun, the God of the Muses, but this meaning should be extended much more widely. As we saw when considering the palm, this finger is served by two nerves of separate origin, one appertaining to the Conscious Self and the other, the Ulna, to the Instinctive or Emotional Self. Think for a moment of real happiness. One can appreciate something intellectually without being moved by it; one can feel the happiness of, say, good health without knowing why, and the feeling is often transient. To be really happy one must appreciate with one or more of the five senses and feel the responding emotion in the Solar Plexus. This is the real happiness which is mirrored by the third finger. The actual form of such meaning may vary from an appreciation of fine art to a business gamble, from a love of the countryside to watching thoroughbreds in competition, the point being that it is that person's idea of his or her happiness.

The total length is in balance when level with the Index finger and about half-way up the nail of Medius. Very long, equal or nearly equal to Saturn, depicts a gambler with life if not with money—the tips will indicate the type. Such a finger takes chances, maybe adventure, maybe lost causes, but the excitement will lure him on and thoughts of worldly wisdom have relatively little weight. The finger may be long but thin and unused in appearance. Here the comparison of the two hands may reveal that all the instincts are towards an artistic pursuit but have been held in abeyance by a strong thumb responding to the demands of Life. When this frustrated finger is seen, it is well to encourage the pursuit of the thwarted dream as a hobby. All too often contrary humans deny themselves the pleasure, the satisfaction of following their gift because if they cannot do it full time it is not worth the bother. This attitude is so mistaken; try to persuade them to use the gift as a hobby at the present, so that it may blossom as a full-time occupation on retirement. 'Ridiculous, what hope has a musician of taking up music at sixty-five?'. Yet because of the unwasted years a village church was blessed with an organist and enthusiastic choirmaster beyond its wildest dreams and all the parish responded to the beautiful music.

When the Apollo finger is short the personality will be

expressed in doing and achieving. The Jupiterian ambitions will dominate with all too little interest in the cultural side of life except, possibly, as a means to an end; but compare the two hands and make quite sure that no part is missing as the result of an injury.

When the length is in the base phalange comfort will play a large part in ideas of happiness: when well supported, a long high-padded base may lead to interior decoration or designing furniture or, when supported by Saturn, designing gardens or golf courses. Whatever the interest, some strong appeal to comfort must be included.

A long middle phalange indicates that the ideas of art must include suitability. Such a formation with a good nail section will appreciate the beauty of cranes against the night sky, or, with the base phalange next in importance, a well-made bath which empties with no puddles. This phalange may be deceptive from the front; when working out possible careers be very careful to measure properly at the side of the finger.

The nail phalange is significant in a cultured society. It mirrors our relation with line, with colour, with craftsmanship and all forms of beauty. A long thin section is associated with an eye for line, while the sturdier form prefers to express itself in colour, but this is a tendency, not a rule. When there is any form of high padding on this finger, especially a 'droplet', accentuated by a high base phalange, the owner will have a keen sense of touch. He may be seen feeling the texture of curtain or garment long after the discussion has moved to size or price, or stroking velvet or cats while thinking of other things.

As in all fingers, Apollo should be straight. I have never seen one wilt towards the little finger, but all too often it wilts towards Saturn, showing that the weight of mundane responsibility has been too strong. No kink in the joint nor holding two fingers together, but just a gentle inclination towards the second, and all too frequently Saturn reciprocates by wilting towards Apollo. This is a psychological defect which should be of interest to psychiatrists, though the basic meaning is really quite simple and, in young people, fairly easy to rectify. The second finger of background and duty is drawn towards happiness, while happiness has a guilty conscience and looks towards duty. This formation is often associated with people who worry about the gas, the children, the home all the time they are out at a party, yet gaze wistfully out of the window when at work. Practical advice which sometimes helps women is to suggest that they keep a definite list of all last-minute duties and check the items, preferably with a companion, before starting out. Duties accomplished and noted in the *Conscious Mind* will stop them worrying. This is only a silly little practical leaven, but it can help to get fingers straighter. Men can play a similar game on leaving work. List the pros and cons or duties for tomorrow and forget them for tonight.

The way this finger is held or put down is revealing and amusing to notice in newspaper photographs. Held closely to the second the idea of happiness clings to the tradition of upbringing, clings to convention; held apart from the second finger it has just the opposite effect, conventions, procedure, rules have but little interest in the search for an independent mind. Among pioneers in Kenya and suchlike places the second and third fingers are so often held together while the little finger stands well away from such dull company. The explanation is that extreme independence of action may be displayed, but always within the tenets of 'the old school tie'.

Tips

The spatulate tip is most at home on this finger; the urge to use the hands can be expressed in art and craftsmanship. The true meaning is a love of life, of movement, in the idea of beauty. Thus it is helpful for an actor as well as a painter or model maker. Think of it as an additional love of life in beauty and the correct ballet will be chosen for an evening out, the correct movie shown on the home cinema. A spatulate third finger equates as beauty in movement, with the highest fulfilment in its owner's own movement.

A *square* tip indicates a good eye for size and proportion. The scope can range from recognizing the number of stitches in a knitted inch to the composition and practical application of artistic creation.

A conic tip is not out of place on the third finger but may

show more appreciation of art than creative instinct. When the phalange is long and well proportioned the conic tip is expressed in a gift for LINE—the cut of clothes, the hang of a curtain, the tapering of a spire appeals to the conic tips of Apollo. The owners can claim useful hands when need arises, but their real flair is the appreciation of the work of others. On a short phalange the interest in art forms will be lacking and the appreciative qualities of the tips may refer to a practical interest in suitability or comfort.

Pointed third fingers are always one of a set and encourage all the ideas and dreams of their pointed companions. Long pointed third finger nail phalanges are in their element in florists' shops, in careers where they have to look beautiful and pay other people to do the hard work. With a strong thumb and suitable finger prints they accomplish much. Without supporting attributes they may inspire ideas in others and have a happy life sampling all the more delightful 'castles in Spain'.

The joint of the nail phalange is important to the pointed tipped Apollo, for if it is smooth ideas will flow smoothly; if knotted, there will be a check between seeing and accepting so that the knot becomes the badge of the critic. The bigger the knot the more devastating the criticism.

Flexibility at this joint suggests that the mind accepts many aspects and varieties of beauty, or, that there is a flair for understanding the meaning underlying the struggle for artistic expression.

The knot of Order at the second joint demands order in beauty. For instance, it may indicate a love of colour blending, harmonies in colour and sound especially when the tip is either spatulate or so nearly spatulate that one has to test with the edge of white paper. I cannot claim many examples of flexibility at the lower joint, except where it just followed the Medius, suggesting that the psychic investigator's idea of happiness lay in variety of approach. I have never seen a third finger with the second joint as the only flexible one on the hand.

Fourth Finger

The fourth, Little or Mercury finger, is to the submerged Self as the first finger is to the conscious Self. A straight Mercury finger ensures straight dealing in accordance with the principles of the owner. With other factors concurring, they are truthful and happier when at peace with themselves. A gentle wilt towards Apollo is known as the finger of sacrifice. People with such fingers will give up their own secret selves to create happiness around them. This condition is found on the hands of those who have to care for other folk. Nurses are frequent possessors, but examples can range from matrons of schools, head waiters, probation officers and ardent secretaries of the R.S.P.C.A. When selecting candidates for such a position of authority, a very gentle slight bend in this finger is a useful indication.

A sharp bend or kink, especially towards the palm, (Fig. 22) is quite different. First make sure that it is not the result of an accident. When natural it is often inherited, but it does suggest that there is some kink in the subconscious character. Any such tendency may be held in check by a good heart and a strong thumb, but a clear, strong kink seems most helpful for anyone contemplating a life of crime. I always blame his beautifully made, straight little finger for the lack of success of a man who, as his wife said, 'was brought up to the burglaring business. Such a good husband and father, I do wish he would give it up.'

Since Mercury is set slightly lower on the palm than the third, it must be checked. To compare it with its neighbour they should both be measured from base line to tip when normal a little finger would come about half-way up the nail phalange of the third finger.

Fig. 22—Kink in Mercury finger

Longer than half-way, it must be considered as Long, and should it be nearly the same length the attributes are accentuated. Mrs. St. Hill said that a long little finger is all the better for twisting people around. This seems to be true, with the proviso that when people refuse to be 'twisted', the long little finger is hurt, it longs to retire into its tent and sulk, but to the owner it is hurt, unwanted, and full of lonely feelings.

That is the negative side of the little finger. On the positive side length goes with intelligence and is often found on the hands of professional and intellectual people.

A Mercury finger that does not attain the nail phalange of its neighbour retains some of the mischievous outlook of a child; a pointed tip increases the wit and mischief. There are some psychological disturbances which have an extreme shortness, but the condition is not necessarily one for psychiatry unless the finger appears to be made of gristle rather than bone. Slightly longer, up to a normal length, the shortness shows speed of thought, the temper is more likely to be outspoken but quickly over, and there is sometimes a lack of patience unless well controlled by other factors.

The base phalange shows our reaction to money as apart from the property aspect inherent in the Saturn finger. Predominating, a base phalange will show a love of money for its own sake, also a gift for acquiring, using and seeing after the cash, as exemplified by the Madame at the desk of a French restaurant. A short, wide section advertises a collecting or hoarding instinct. One is often told that this reading is incorrect—'I was cured of hoarding when I . . . had to move . . . married a soldier' . . . and so on. Wait, and before long a little cache of plates, of boxes and boxes of pins, of string (to quote only three of many) will show how alive the instinct remains despite rigid control.

The second phalange habitually is the shortest, but when as long as one of the others, or longer than the base one, there will be a capacity for retaining interest in a task until completion. Tasks can be finished by will power, but length in this middle section shows a true gift for enjoying the doing all the way through. This peculiarity is frequently found on hands that are used in scientific work where interest has to be maintained over long periods.

Extreme shortness, even to the disappearance of the second phalange with the two joints merged as one, is exemplified by Dr. Wolff in her work on the mentally retarded. A notable shortness of the section indicates an inability to sort and co-ordinate ideas. I suggest that less than half the length of either phalanges would constitute such shortness.

The nail phalange shows the power of receiving and expressing ideas, whether in speech or writing, so that ideally it should be appreciably longer than either of the others and should look well and finely made, when it will be expressive of a keen intelligence. A short section, especially on a child's hands, makes teaching difficult and almost impossible for the child to express any ideas he has.

In most British hands Mercury is held well apart from the other fingers, asserting the independence of spirit which leads to actions performed, as we saw from Apollo, in the most decorous way. The wider apart it is held the more surprising the actions may be. Held close to the others it is a sign of restriction. Without mentioning what you have seen, ask the client to shake the hand and put it down again naturally. If Mercury still clings to its neighbours, the indication of some over-training or over-control is correct, and the cause should be sought so as to alleviate, or at least face, the condition if possible. Chinese hands are often portrayed with the fingers close together, but I do not know if the precepts of Confucius still influence thought. Religious orders tend to encourage fingers held together, not only in prayer but as a usual gesture, which would stress 'Not my will but Thine be done'—the instinctive Self under strict control.

There is occasionally a mishap to the tendons of the little finger which draws it down on to the palm. As this seems to promise to be the result of a trace element deficiency, be careful not to see it as a psychological development.

Tips

The tip of the little finger is usually more pointed than the others, and since points give ideas and speed of thought this form is in its highest expression here. A rather short, pointed Mercury adds a gift of mimicry to the wit, but I would stress that it shows the wit of the brain and not the type of humour which can see the jest against itself. A conic tip enjoys some humour too, but is not as quick or as witty as the other form.

Square tips are only found on the fourth finger as one of a set, and even then are often more conic than the rest of the hand. This blend can lead to a sharp, clever form of expression but there is a tendency, the more nearly it approximates to the square, for it to express itself in doing rather than saying.

Spatulate little fingers are sometimes found in company with just the third finger of this type; they are craftsmen expressing themselves in making things. With both joints knotted the spatulate type make wonderful organizers with every detail in order. The knots make good organizers with any type of tip, but the spatulate gives them more scope.

Flexibility at the top joint is under observation by the S.S.P.P. We have reason to think that it indicates sharp hearing, as for the bell of a distant telephone perhaps, or the squeak of bats. Owners, when asked, are inclined to deny it, thinking of accuracy of ear or true pitch, which is the domain of the Mount of Venus. Then one has to wait for information until some sound is made which may be picked up by the dog and the owner of the flexible finger.

I have no comment about a flexible lower joint, as this remains to be studied.

Smooth fingers follow the rule that they are a sign of speed of intuition and are of great assistance to the long pointed first phalange in assimilating and expressing thoughts.

Setting (on palm)

As we saw (page 32) little fingers may be set on the palm much below the level of the other fingers. When the lower joint of the Mercury finger is level with the palm beneath the other fingers, a very strong sense of self-distrust is present. It differs from the inferiority complex of the low first finger by being much deeper. One mistrusts oneself, sometimes com-

pensating by being rather dominant towards the world and
co-workers. The owners are always checking their own
statements, looking up in dictionary or encyclopaedia before
speaking, measuring, making certain, because outside criticism
and their own mistakes make them curl up with a tension they
cannot alleviate. The low-set little finger may be 'just like
mother's', as it is such a noticeable aspect of heredity. Fig. 57,
page 238 is a good example.

Never miss an opportunity of commending; help them
towards their own self-confidence, and in young hands the
little finger may rise to a normal position.

The other extreme, when the fingers are all level as in
Egyptian drawings or the Tudor arch, is exactly opposite
in meaning. The high set Mercury is quite certain of its own
infallibility and expects the world to agree.

The happy position for the line of the fourth finger is to
be just about one-third of the base section lower than the
third finger.

CHAPTER IV

THUMB

THE WHOLE hand is ruled by the thumb which is the key to behaviour. By its opposition to the fingers the thumb has the grip and ability to use tools. From that ability has been developed the power to reason and to look ahead.

A thumb is an essentially human development and portrays far more than the common urge to get one's own way. Monkeys can try for that objective with their weak, gristle thumbs as they snatch a banana or cuff their companions. The power shown by human thumbs lies in our ability to use reasoned desire—to hold the objective in our own minds. People with poor thumbs will join the monkeys in running after any 'bit of banana', the last bit to be thrown. Thumbs are usually defined as showing 'will-power' but the more correct definition is that 'Thumbs measure the power of purposeful direction'.

Length

The thumb is measured from the tip to the line of attachment to the palm, under the Index finger. There are two schools of thought about the ideal length, neither wholly satisfactory. One demands that it is the same length as the little finger, thus ensuring balance to the five digits. Another theory is that it should attain half-way up the base phalange of the Index finger when the digits are held together. There is such variety in the angle of attachment to the palm, giving such differences of space between their respective bases, that

a very long thumb, when low set, may not appear to attain
the half-way mark.

For a 'good' thumb I ask that the nail phalange should
be the longest section on the hand by a good measure. For a
rough guide, say twenty-five per cent longer than the longest
of the finger sections; this will ensure its human command over
the fingers.

Third

The third, lowest phalange of the thumb is incorporated in
the Mount of Venus which, we remember, represents our
feeling for Life. To feel alive makes one want to DO, to express
oneself. Before putting any determination into action one must
feel a desire to do so; the Mount of Venus, when considered
as the base of the thumb, represents 'Desire'.

Second

The next step is to think how to obtain or execute that
desire. This ability is gauged by the middle phalange which
gives away a great deal about our habitual method of approach.
When long, as long as the nail section, it suggests much time
may be expended on reasoning out the modus operandi—
preferably in talking about it. When the middle phalanges
are appreciably longer than the top one reasoning will be so
dominant that action is precluded.

When short, action will be founded on instinct or intuition
with a minimum of deliberation.

Should the whole hand bespeak intelligence with a good
Mercury finger, the owner of a short middle phalange justifies
the action later, if and when necessary; action may be in
response to long and arduous training, but the speed of
decision does not permit lengthy recapitulation.

Do not argue, except in fun, with a very short middle
section, as argument will be taken for obtuseness, but the
owner of a long section will thoroughly enjoy burning the
midnight oil in discussion.

The middle phalange may have a thick or waisted appearance. Picture the reasoning power being passed, as it were,
through a sieve. When the mesh is fine so that the thumb is

waisted the Reason will emerge graceful and accommodating, manifesting as instinctive tact. When the sieve is coarse and the thumb looks thick, it lacks such refining influence; the owner cannot see why anything that is reasonable and true should need 'dressing-up'. This is especially noticeable in a long phalange which is also thick, when the discussion may be reiterated over and over again, while action waits.

The Nail Phalange is as ever, the flowering, the performance and mirrors the Power. It can be argued that the ideal thumb would show both sections of equal length but the more successful hands have the nail phalange at least a little the longer.

To assess how the determination will be carried into effect

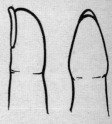

Fig. 23—Spoke-shaved tip   Fig. 24—Pointed tip

one has only to look at the shape of this nail phalange; the very appearance will warn in what manner the will operates. The longer the phalange the more determined the Will, or the more controlled the desires. The finer it is the more graceful any application of the Will, until the ultra fine, 'spoke-shaved' tip that looks as though the fleshy part had been sharpened into the nail shows the person who can get his or her own way without anyone noticing—the tip seems to work its way between the bricks of opposition (Fig. 23).

Pointed tips often ornament long nail phalanges and have a wonderful capacity for getting their own way. No one resents them for they assert their wishes so diplomatically and say 'Thank-you' so prettily—but what they want is done. If such a tip should be on a poor phalange of course the effect is minimized but it still seems to operate gracefully. There is a difference of approach between the tip which is pointed across the pad (Fig. 24) and the 'spoke-shaved' which is pointed into the nail. The true pointed tip is quick to see openings, to use ideas, while the spoke-shaved form can add diplomacy to any shape of tip.

Conic thumbs have the feeling of both worlds, of ideas and utility, but with this shape, not being ultra decisive in itself, the effect depends more on the size and shape of the whole thumb.

Square tips to the thumbs have the usual quality of care and justice. The formation is of frequent occurrence even on hands that have few of the fingers square tipped. The effect seems to be a balance, an instinctive flair for justice, which is of great help in their dealings with other men.

Spatulate thumbs are the sign of craftsmen in some form. Everyone knows the 'Potter's' thumb with its width and pads of sensitive feeling; sculptors and painters are apt to have the same pattern in lesser degree, while a few instinctive specimens can usually be found in an engineering workshop or garage.

Clubbed, a coarse, heavy tip to the thumb indicates a bludgeon-like attack. The extreme of this formation is called

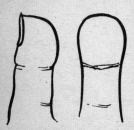

the 'Murderer's thumb' and suggests that in the event of opposition the owner will want to use his fists. This formation affects the whole of the top of the phalange rather than just the tip as in a spatulate thumb. It might be seen as the antithesis of the spoke-shaved.

When identified on an otherwise charming pair of hands the inter-pretation needs much consideration.

Fig. 25—Clubbed

On one hand only, the heavy top may be traced back to a

privateer ancestor or a line of Border Barons. I once found a pair belonging to a kind and gentle man of the Law; when I was commenting on this discrepancy his friend inquired 'Have you ever seen him in Court?' and substantiated the capacity for ruthlessness. Yet another pair on the hands of a woman equally high-minded, she drove *herself* to her chosen task to the exclusion of all other considerations. When a child is born with this clubbed thumb try to salt the effect with self-control, with consideration for others and humour, that it may grow up as charming and use the attribute as well as the daughter of the pirate.

A thumb can acquire a deformed shape through constant sucking which is not a wise habit when the child grows up to six or seven years old with the thumb always in its mouth. Often starting with a feeling of insecurity, the habit, when firmly fixed, is very difficult to dislodge. When little Miss Six-Year-Old begins to take an interest in her appearance, showing her the ultimate hideousness of her thumb as seen on another hand, may stop the habit through shock, and the thumb squeezed back into shape instead of being sucked.

Fig. 26
Stubborn

There is a firm 'Law' that width shows resistant Will even as length shows executive Will. When a long, well-shaped thumb swells on the nail side of the joint (Fig. 26.) the owner has the potentiality to achieve success in a self-employed or otherwise responsible position. The length allows him to decide on a course and carry it out while the width enables him to hold on through adversity until a better opportunity presents itself.

A short wide phalange suggests that the power within the personality is not exerted until fully aroused in self-defence. 'Live and let live' is their motto—they just will not be ordered about.

When this resistant or stubborn type of thumb is associated with a pronounced, outstanding joint between the second phalange and the Mount of Venus (Fig 11) an exceptionally accurate sense of timing may be expected; the thumb will wait until just the right moment to make the supreme effort to accomplish the objective. This sense of order in Time was described with the Thenar eminence (page 26).

A flexible thumb may be seen even when the rest of the hand shows no such tendency. The attributes of a bending back thumb are an important guide when working with other people. A thumb can bend backwards at either of its joints.

When the lower, Order in Time, joint is flexible, sometimes called 'double-jointed', there is a weakness between desire and reason. These people are apt to feel they cannot be bothered to pursue a wish or course of conduct opposed to the convenience of other people. In one form of behaviour they give up far too easily for their own good, and think they are being nobly unselfish. This double joint often accompanies a very strong upper part to the thumb so that once they are convinced of the rightness of a proposed action, especially if it is a 'Cause', they will show astonishing determination.

There can be another aspect to this weakness between desire and reason, often endorsed by a poor first phalange of the thumb. The 'easiest way' is so attractive that the gratification leads to selfishness or self-indulgence which is quite unrecognized. Doing that which appears most attractive at the moment is not conducive to an ordered, successful life. One has met so many hands with this double joint whose owners have so often done foolish things in business or domestic relations, taken the easiest way, that now I tell them they must do one deliberately selfish action each day—like a boy scout in reverse—to get into a habit of being firm and not too self-abnegating when such conditions arise. When the motives are not so pure, making oneself take a clear decision and perform it each day may still be a beneficial exercise.

First joint. A thumb which bends back at the upper joint has flexibility between reason, the power of thinking, and performance. The owner can make up his mind and grasp opportunities as they present themselves. It is as well to take no notice of the various adjectives which may be applied to this flexibility because the owner may be wildly generous one day and incredibly mean when in pursuit of some other interest. The capacity to bend back is invaluable to people who have to switch their minds from one subject to another. A peculiar characteristic is that these people like to work in cycles. They will be enthusiastic over A; then they cannot bear to work at A and plunge into B. Perhaps they will evolve an interest in C before they return to subject A with fresh enthusiasm, even inspiration. Their cycle may be reckoned in months or extend to a year or so, the rhythm may be influenced by circumstances but it will be their own, personal rhythm. Again, circumstances may compel them to catch the 8.15 train every morning, but the 6.45 one morning and the 9.20 another day will vastly increase their happiness and health.

Sometimes a thumb appears to bend back at the upper joint but upon examination the joint itself is found to be stiff with only the actual nail phalange bending backwards. These are the people who keep their determination as a steady steel shaft but vary the approach so that their colleagues think an idea has been dropped and forgotten—unless the colleagues happen to realize that the process being carried out is exactly the proposition which was turned down six months previously. In effect this bending back of the tip is closely allied to the 'spoke-shaved' tip but there is a subtle difference between the deliberate diplomacy of the finely pointed rapier and the approach from a new angle to achieve the persistence of determination mirrored in the stiff joint.

A really stiff thumb is the signal of Persistence, the owners of such thumbs enjoy the 8.15 train and would be miserable if it left without them. They can keep diaries, do daily exercises, keep to a diet, all things a bending thumb tries so hard to do and drops at the end of a week. Their foible is that they cannot recognize Opportunity when she knocks on their door unless that elusive lady comes in the habit of an expected, worked-for advancement.

This stiff formation must not be confused with either stubbornness or obstinacy, it is amenable to reason and can make changes after due deliberation.

Fig. 27
Persistent

To pay this persistent thumb just tribute I must stress that one finds it on the hands of many people who have risen to positions of responsibility and authority in their own sphere of life.

Stubbornness may be defined as the capacity to maintain one's own opinion despite advice, persuasion or argument but that decision or opinion is founded upon reasoned conviction.

Obstinacy is the maintaining of a position because one has said so and cannot be overcome even by one's own conviction and/or wishes; it is the last defence of naturally weak-willed folk. Stubbornness is shown by the thumb which widens on the nail side of the joint (Fig. 26). The obstinate thumb (Fig. 28) is recognized by an enlarged and knotted top joint. Be certain of feeling the joint itself by flexing and straightening the thumb. This thickness shows a barrier between Reason and Will.

Fig. 28
Obstinate

When one has to work with a pair of such thumb joints the easiest way is to ask the owner which he wishes of possible alternatives, there may be wisdom in making one's own preferred path seem slightly less desirable, but argument is useless—find a way round, a new and apparently irrelevant approach may offer face-saving encouragement.

Angle of Opening. Note how the thumb opens away from the hand, and how nearly it approximates to a right-angle with the fingers. Indian teaching* sees the perfectly balanced soul in a thumb which opens at exactly ninety degrees (Fig. 29) but such openings are rare especially in both hands. Most people have cares and inhibitions which make them carry the thumb at a more acute angle to the fingers. Should it open, as do the thumbs of children, at a wider angle than ninety degrees there will be an adventurous absence of restraint.

A thumb that is held tightly against the fingers, even when the hand is shaken loose and put down again, indicates some strain or tension which has become an habitual way of facing

* Mir Bashir's lectures to S.S.P.P. 1948

C

life. This tension can become free again with happiness.

Position of Rotation. The thumb rotates at the wrist joint as anyone can see by moving their own from between the stretched open position to the gripping position against the finger pads. The place on the arc in which it is habitually held reveals the owner's attitude to himself.

Remembering that the thumb is the primary sign of the

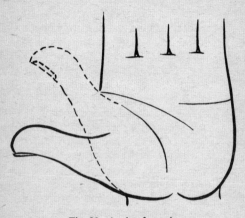

Fig. 29—Angle of opening

human species, and that the grip of thumb against fingers has given Man all the power over Nature that he possesses, the meaning of its position can be visualized readily.

When aligned with the fingers so that nearly all the nail can be seen from the back when the hand is held up, (Fig. 30), the Will is the servant of any wishes or spheres of interest suggested by the fingers. All suggestions will be carried out with enthusiasm.

Should the thumb appear to be almost facing the fingers with, at most, only a third of the nail visible from the back (Fig. 31), it is a sign of self-control: possibly natural when on both hands equally, but more often enforced by circumstances. I call it a Sergeant-Major on parade to those fingers. Self-control may become a fetish, so look for accompanying signs of conflict on the lines of the palm.

These are the two extremes; a comfortable, good citizen angle allows about one-third of the nail to be visible from the front, while the angle of order in Time does not work

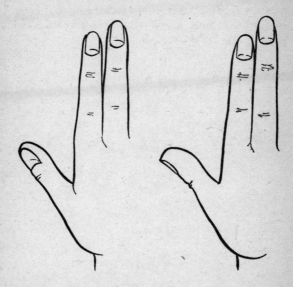

Fig. 30—Thumb aligned with fingers   Fig. 31—Thumb opposing fingers

round to the front of the palm but remains identifiable when the hand is held open.

The difference between the tightly held thumb and the 'Sergeant-Major' angle illustrates the difference between inhibition and self-control. The former is an inward clenching of the mind and soul, the latter a determination to be master of one's self but deliberately, not from a sense of guilt but from self-respect—the body and mind are disciplined that the soul may be free.

Position on Palm. A thumb which appears to be placed high on the palm, a long way from the wrist as in the monkey hands, belongs to someone with originality. It may be seen as sharing in the thoughts shown by the fingers, but the thoughts arise from within.

The opposite extreme, one which appears to start directly from the wrist itself, has to have a key of some sort to start the inspiration. A composer may hear the song of a bird, a writer builds up from some trifling incident in the newspaper, perhaps Sir Isaac Newton would have had this low set thumb from his response to the famous apple.

CHAPTER V

BACK OF THE HAND

WHEN A student is familiar with the principles of Chirognomy the back of the hand will be observed first. An instructive lesson may be appreciated during any period of waiting, in Press photographs, on meeting people for the first time and in dealing with people who are in any position of authority. Having decided to what manner of person such hands may belong a fascination lies in watching whether first impressions are supported by behaviour.

It is difficult to lay down an order of observation because, having learnt to notice the various parts until the recognition is instinctive, one takes in the hand as a whole.

From the back one notices the colour of skin; colour, shape and texture of nails; flexibility of the joints and whether smooth or knotted; relative length of fingers; here too it is easy to assess the shape of tips but both tips and relative length of fingers should be verified on turning the hand over to study the palm. All these details build up into a revealing picture of the person before he has noticed that he is being inspected.

Colour of Skin

A quick glance shows whether the skin is of a normal pink, camellia white, sun-burnt, or out-of-doors rough.

The ultra white skin is basically self-centred. It is as though there is an extra self-protective skin to cut off contact with the world. This egocentricity may be controlled by a strong thumb and a good heart line together with other linear indications, but the very kindnesses often reflect back to the advantage of the owner of the camellia skin. Palmists can never understand why white hands are so extolled in poetry and suspect that the ladies kept their swains dancing like infatuated marionettes.

Nice, warm, human colour has no such obsession and can reflect whatever the rest of the hand may indicate.

Very dark, out-of-door hands are usually the result of weather and tell of an outdoor type of man or woman. Hands often look blue in cold weather, but when that is their habitual colour it bespeaks a poor circulation. Sometimes the poverty of the blood supply makes the owner lack energy that he cannot carry out the promise of the rest of the hand. Except for the warning of the white skin the chief interest of colour is in relation to occupation, hobbies and health.

Texture of Skin

The texture of skin should also be noted. A fine skin shows a subdued pattern of fibres and is normally accompanied by a fine net-work of lines.

Coarse graining on the back of the hand anticipates few lines on the palm—a 'man of tougher fibre'. In older books stress is laid on the hairiness of hands, but except for observing whether the texture of hair harmonizes with the texture of skin I have not found any particular warning or attribute. If coarse, stiff hair grows out of fine textured skin, there may be a warning of conflicting inheritances to be questioned on the palm. Soft hair growing out of coarse skin may be on the genetic path towards a hairless condition.

Age should be gauged from the wrinkled skin on the back of a hand. This is not always easy to do because fat people with soft hands retain the smooth stretch of skin until late in life. Fat does not always lodge on the hands; there are large, portly but energetically minded people with lean, bony or muscular hands which can wrinkle very much with age. Despite many theories I think one can only decide on the broadest basis of young, not-so-young or definitely old. But, always beware of the immediate effect of detergents and exposure.

Knuckles

As we saw from the palmar side, any knots at joints give a pause, a slowness, which enables order to be observed.

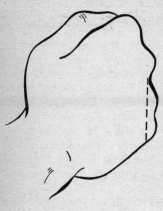

Fig. 32—Knuckles

Knuckles are at the Material end of the fingers so they signify order in material things, i.e. tidiness. Note that they represent the standard of tidiness of the wearer. A not over-clean shirt and jeans may be surmounted by an exact pattern of whisker side-boards. The capacity for more conventional tidiness will emerge as the age of soaplessness ceases to be fashionable.

First finger. A pronounced joint at the first finger will indicate that the interest in tidiness is in relation to the self, clothes and personal things will be well appointed.

At the second finger the accent will be on home and/or office. There will be an appreciation of neatness shown in all their belongings or surroundings.

The third finger bone prominent shows a gift for making everything look nice when finished. Without it things may be beautifully made, ponies thoroughly well educated, but the final polish is almost impossible to achieve without infinite thought and care. Even with the care someone with a well-developed joint saunters up and in two flicks adds the perfect finish.

The little finger knuckle shows the instinctive love of, or gift for, tidiness. 'I can't go to bed with my room unfinished' says an over-weary pronounced little finger knuckle after a fourteen- or sixteen-hour day moving house. So, when working with them, get a superficial neatness to their surroundings even though all your work may have to be redone on the morrow.

Among young people the instinct towards tidiness may be

submerged in the need for haste but will re-appear when occasion allows.

The two joints above the knuckles were studied in Chapter III but once their implications are clearly recognized it is often easier to appreciate knots and flexibility from the back of the hands so that one may decide how the hands are to be read when they are turned over.

The length of the phalanges are noted from the back of the hand by some Chirologists who achieve excellent results. I prefer to make certain by measurement on the palmar side. However, a strikingly long base phalange often indicates a sailor or someone who enjoys travelling. That is not a rule, but an amusing guess for, say, a railway journey.

The way the hand is put down, distances between fingers and their normal spread can also be seen better from the back and how much the fingers curl inwards or lie flat and relaxed, all these clues may be followed as a matter of interest on the hands of strangers.

Tips whether square or spatulate can also be judged from the relation to the sides of the nails.

NAILS

Normally the eye is first attracted by the nails. They are generally accepted as an indication of health and temper. When the famous Dr. Geikie Cobb had pneumonia very badly he noticed his own nails turning black, only resuming their normal colour as he recovered. As a result of his observation he cleared the stigma from the study of nails as a supplement to his original work on the endocrine system.

When measuring the size of a nail consider only the pink, alive part and the shape of base and sides—not the end that can be shaped by the manicurist.

Also note the moons, whether they are of suitable size, too large, or non-existent. Moons are often taken as indicative of health but their absence may be the result of some pre-natal condition. Absence of moon is often found on the nails of people thoroughly tough in constitution. On the other hand moons which have been present and later disappear are not a good sign, they may be an early warning of the onslaught of one of the rheumatic family of organic ill-health. Ultra large moons are thought, by some practitioners, to be a sign of heightened vitality. I have no proof, and though moons indicate the area of growth for the nail there is no certainty that abnormal growth of nails or hair is a healthy sign.

A nicely shaped, clearly edged moon is so much more pleasing to the eye that one instinctively endows it with virtue to which I am not sure the nail itself is entitled.

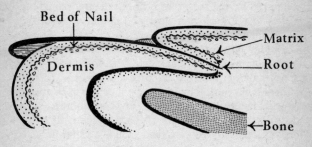

Fig. 33—Structure of nail

Construction

That nails are imbedded in the skin and flesh of the finger, from the hidden root, along the sides, and under the surface of the horn, is so obvious that one never thinks about it. Translated into a colony of specialized cells, working like proverbial beavers at making the root or matrix, their colleagues forming the nerve endings, ducts and capillaries, feeding, pushing, encouraging the passage of the sheath of horn so that blemishes and injuries grow out, wear is compensated, the whole thing renewed approximately within six months—there is a miracle which demands our recognition.

All these groups of cells need sustenance and special food to make the 'Kerastin' which hardens the horn, so that any deviations from good health will affect them in some measure. The endocrine system plays a large part in this food supply, supported by a generous mineralization in which must be included calcium to make them hard, silica and a trace of arsenic to make them clear, etc. The substance Kerastin, which is responsible for the difference between nail and skin and hair, is an albumoid in which are three amino acids—tyrosine, tryptophane and cystin, the last is the acid which is rich in sulphur and short of oil, and controls the hardness of the horn. There are also small but vital quantities of mineral trace elements.

The late M. Henri Mangin, a Chirologist of international repute, made a most detailed study of nails which he gathered into his book *Étude Clinique et Psychologique des Ongles*. His findings for the most part bear out the traditional meanings assigned to the various shapes and colours but he suggested basic reasons.

Chirology has, for some time, associated the first phalanges or nail sections of the fingers with the endocrine system, and this work of M. Mangin confirms the physical basis for the empirical belief; the glandular system being, in its turn, associated with health and temperament. The tradition of temper and health indications being assigned to the nails is therefore borne out and may be considered reliable as far as it goes. So much more research is needed on the subject that I have only here discussed, as fully as possible, what is known.

Standards

The perfect nail has parallel sides. The length from cuticle to quick, the border of the alive, coloured part, should measure half the total length of the nail phalange. It should appear smooth, shiny and, among the white races, of a delicate pink colour which harmonizes with the surrounding skin. When a hand is sunburnt or naturally dark as in African races the colour should match the palm. (There are exceptions to the pink palmed Negroid race as at least one tribe in Central Africa has dark palms, but my impression of the two examples I saw was that the nails were rather darker too.)

The moons should be milky in colour, clearly defined and about one-fifth of the length of the nail. Nails may be square or rectangular as long as they follow the shape of the fingers.

With a perfect nail Mangin looks for a temperament to match—'balanced, controlled, reasonable and sane, able to take a wide view with a clarity of ideas'.

Varieties

There are many deviations from perfection and each has its own story to tell:—

There are large square nails, to tiny squares, hardly to be called nails.

There are long nails, from rectangular through various degrees of narrowness to the shape of a date stone.

There are shell-shaped nails and Chinese fan-shaped.

There are all shades of colour from carmine red through rose to white; blemishes of yellow, brown, blue to black: lines and borders of various colours; a yellow or brownish tinge would infer liver trouble as when the whites of the eyes appear to have a yellow tinge. There may be white spots, red spots, black spots.

There are soft nails, hard, brittle, tough, inward curving, or dish shaped, also various deformities which are sometimes inherited peculiarities.

To each and all M. Mangin ascribes a particular meaning of health and temperament, but here they will be grouped as much as possible, from my own experience, so that the readings may be simplified without losing any aspect of truth.

Colour

Colour first attracts the eye. The horny part of the nail being a semi-transparent window through which is seen the state of the tissues beneath, the meaning is obvious. Carmine red reveals an over zealous blood supply, 'hot-blooded'; while the pale to white nail is cold and restricted.

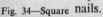

Large square nails are slow to anger but involve the solar-plexus in their emotion, often feeling sick after they have been compelled to anger. They feel measured temper, i.e. righteous wrath. When coloured red or a generous pink the wrath will be expressed; the same shape in white will put the wrath on ice to be remembered for all time. Forgiveness is not a quality much practised by large, white, square nails.

Fig. 34—Square

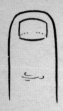

Fig. 35—Square (small)

A very tiny square nail is not well nurtured so there is a meagre narrowness of ideas, they show a lack of warmth, of love, often restricted sex which may lead to narrow, restricted jealousies. Mangin associates them with narrowness to fanaticism in religion but this I cannot confirm. Small square nails do not easily allow themselves to be shown to a Chirologist. They have the certitude of righteousness without the capacity to understand or to judge fairly. It must be remembered that any pattern on a hand is only one ingredient of the character and may be controlled or adapted by the influence of the other ingredients.

Fig. 36—Filbert

The narrow, long, filbert shape shows a lack of energy at its root so the temper is gentle: these subjects prefer not to waste their vitality in unpleasurable emotion. As long as there is no blemish on the nails the health is in no way affected, but they have the instinct to conserve their energies as they tend to 'live on their nerves'. Filbert nails encourage an overlong little finger to sulk.

Fig. 37—Date stone

The extreme, date stone shape is starved of all the good contributions from the glandular system, often a poor arterial system, and in ill health may become neurotic. Sometimes this 'date stone' pattern is on only one finger when it may be the result of an accident in youth or a hereditary peculiarity.

Fig. 38—Almond

Between the two extremes is the almond shape so much admired by writers and painters, a convention in Royal portraiture that leaves a nagging query in the mind when studying portraits in the National Portrait Gallery. To Mangin they show—'a sensitive nature, devoted, generous, courteous, naturally distinguished and refined, with a gentleness of character in harmony with aesthetic tendencies'. Display of temper largely follows the colour but they feel anger from the nerves rather than from emotion, more irritability than wrath.

When any of the narrow nails are of poor quality, lined, brittle, or flexible, health and diet should be investigated; if possible biochemistry checked, as their owners may not be as robust as one would wish. In several cases the nails were protesting about neglected meals and/or sleep—as with girls sharing flats together and too busy to cook.

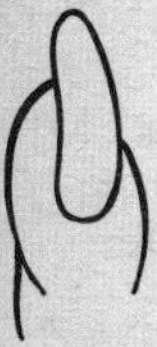

Fig. 39—Talon

When narrow nails are tough in texture, sometimes almost tubular, they can grow like talons and are often quite red. They are so tough that they can be manicured so that the white part is nearly as long as the pink. When yellow or brown tinged, the owners suffer from constipation, while the fingers are often held at rest markedly in-curving too. I have found that with these claw-like nails there is a talon-like ruthlessness to grab and to hold; often with much superficial charm that hides the undeviating possessiveness. They are able to act a display of temper to gain their own ends, but in their hearts they do not feel any emotion except calculated determination to win.

Wide nails.

Fig. 40
Wide

Fig. 41
Wide (small)

Wide nails show a quick temper and are frequently short in relation to the finger pad. Again the colour measures the amount of energy so that a red nail, appreciably wider from side to side than its length, will long to use its fists when angry. Even the paler forms show their anger but wide nails never bear malice.

Fig. 42—Shell

Among the wide nail-forms the opposite extreme of the healthy wide nail is the shell shape. This goes with an ultra sensitive nervous system, often hasty by instinct. Nails can alter to this shell shape after a stroke or other serious affliction of the nervous system; balance and power of assimilation has gone from the matrix and, in older people, the nail itself suffers degenerative streaks up the horn and friability The shell can appear on the hands of younger people with overwork from examinations for scholarships, etc. They signal that when the strain is over the young people should be encouraged to have a holiday on a farm, or some activity which will draw them to the healing of Mother Earth.

Mixed shapes of nails on a pair of hands are quite normal with each finger advertising its relation to people, to background, to art. A long, narrow filbert on the little finger illustrates the plea of the poor German Count in 'The Caravanners' ('Elizabeth and her German Garden') who 'woke up quite good tempered and would have remained so all day had not . . .'

Curving nail. Normally a nail should have a very slight, springy-looking curve from root to tip. Variations suggest disruptions of health rather than character except in so far as off-perfect health does affect one's reactions.

Fig. 43
Hippocratic

The extreme example of the too rounded nail is known as the 'Hippocratic' which that famous Greek observed as a swelling up of the nail and tissues at the end of the fingers, especially the Index.. He attributed the condition to consumption. This is a recognized medical symptom even now, but there is a divergence of opinion as to the basic cause and meaning which I should prefer to discuss in detail, with examples, in Chapter IV, Part Four, page 231 as it is a subject demanding medical investigation.

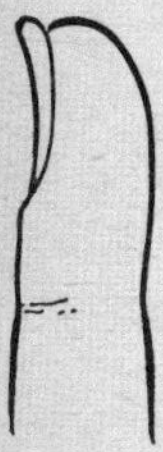

Dished. Sometimes nails dip on their journey from moon to tip and become so concave that they form a sort of dish. This again may follow mineral imbalance, but by starvation, an inadequate supply of blood causing shrinking of the substance under the nail horn. This dishing may happen when the nervous system is affected. M. Mangin does not rule out alcoholism but I have not found the dished condi-

Fig. 44—Dished tion on the few Alcoholics, both practising and members of A.A., whose hands I have known. In at least two of the subjects the nails were particularly well formed. Possibly this condition is found when the craving is caused by mineral deficiencies and might be an indication of the direction of the needed help. One set of dished nails became accentuated after Blackwater fever.

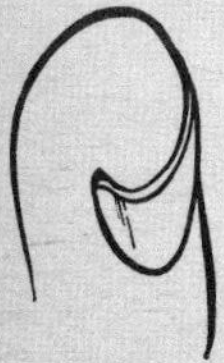

Fig. 45—Injury
to vertebrae

Peculiarities

When any abnormality is seen on one finger only but *not* on the thumb there will be some history of accident to the root so that the horn actually grows out at an untrue angle—like naturally wavy hair. When the pattern is repeated on the thumb the finger in question may be drawing attention to the part of the organism over which it presides, with the resultant danger to vitality. (Fig. 45.) For instance, in an example of injury to Vertebrae. The nail of the Medius fingers, when viewed from the cutting end, grew a sharp corner or downwards angle. This abnormality was most marked on the side of the nail corresponding with the side of the spine affected by the injury. Thumbs, in this case, were not involved as vitality was not impaired.

Spots

White spots are more frequent in some areas of the country than in others. They are often seen in the New Forest where there is a marked calcium deficiency. They are also frequent on the hands of growing children. Sometimes the spots remain for the whole journey of the sheath, sometimes disappear as suddenly as they arrived. There is a theory that a bubble of oxygen has become imprisoned under the nail thus impairing the transparency, which is probably the cause of the temporary spots. My own experience attributes the permanent white spots to lack of calcium, probably in the phosphate form of that essential mineral.

Red spots are the result of a blob of blood becoming incorporated in the horn—possibly due to an unnoticed accident.

Black spots first start as blue, turning darker as they merge and spread over the nail, as observed by Dr. Geikie Cobb.

When the spots become so numerous as to combine in cloud-like layers across the nail, usually at the outgrowing end, about half-way from the moon, the situation is exaggerated. The condition may be due to the work on which the hands are employed having an influence on the grease necessary for the horn.

CHAPTER VI

GESTURE

SINCE HANDS are in the closest possible communication with the brain, passing emotions and thoughts will show their traces despite the axiom of childhood—'Don't fidget'. The variety of movement is infinite but let us look at a few typical examples:

Watch as a person comes towards you; hands hanging loosely at the side denoting tiredness of body or mind. Hands may be clenched with determination or fingers entwined in apprehensive nervousness. Dickens saw hand washing with invisible soap as a sign of hypocrisy when he made that a frequent gesture of Uriah Heep; but it can be a form of nervousness by someone who does want to be a success in your eyes. There is a gesture as of trying to wipe some influence off the hands, possibly the subject's own emotions, when one hand almost milks the other fingers. Of course the last two examples might be alternatives to rubbing briskly when cold!

The normal standard has the fingers curling-in lightly with no muscular effort, arms free but alive, moving with the rhythm of the body but 'belonging' not just hanging by themselves.

Shaking Hands

The feel of a hand in greeting is revealing too. The normal, balanced person gives a pleasant, alive feeling without trying to squash one's fingers into a solid hoof. Suspect the too hearty grip when given by anyone except a very extrovert, Martian type of person full of the joy of physical well-being. The really strong hand is usually gentle. When a 'sports-type' woman lunges at you and grips your hand as though catching a cricket ball, her gesture may well be camouflage, a signal of attempted compensation for all she feels she has lost in femininity: I always study those hands as closely and understandingly as I can.

Everyone knows the 'warm' handshake, the extra pressure with a soulful look into the eyes which is self-evident of the sex-symbol by man or woman. This is a recognized technique and not to be confused with the lingering prelude to holding-hands which is likely to be sincere, at least at the moment.

Weak, flabby, fish-like handshakes can come from either a lack of robustness in health—just too much effort to contact another person, or they can be a sign of egoism—let other people do the work while the owner directs or demands. This self-centred attitude is divulged by only the fingers being involved in the gesture, the palm remains aloof. This egotistical greeting used to be given with the hand held rather high but that fashion has passed.

When Dr. Debrunner was assisting the Swiss Army in the assessment of suitability for promotion to commissioned rank he told the candidates to hold their hands level with their faces that he might photograph both together. The way the hands were held up was a revealing indication of the man's attitude. There were hands held straight up each side of the face, some palm forward, some with the backs to the camera. Both are natural gestures but perhaps those who concealed the palm were better adapted for the Intelligence or Special branches One pair was held with the fingers stiffly together, knuckles bent at right-angles stiffly pointing at his own head. Some were clenched in defence or aggression and so on.

This can be an amusing and revealing game to try in a group of friends when the gestures will lead to discussion on the whole subject of hands and gestures.

On Using Hands

Many years ago a young surgeon told me how irritated he was when instruments were offered in a series of jerks. To pick up an object and offer it in one smooth movement is a sign of self-control. Even if it is the wrong offering at least the recipient can see if it is or is not what he needs. When given in a series of nervous jerks the idea of incorrectness arrives before the object. A smooth, purposeful gesture can hide a lack of self-confidence so well that the gesture itself inspires confidence in other minds.

Some people think that only races born in a sunny clime can use their hands in talk. Certainly their gestures are more unrestricted, more explanatory; often one does not need to know the language to follow directions or follow the gist of a conversation. Northern people need more careful observation but that is the first step towards accurate Chirology. The old-fashioned test of asking for a description of a spiral staircase will prove the correctness of the claim that everyone does use the hand in explanation.

Television is a fruitful source of interest for the observation of gesture if only the camera would not wander away to enlarge a face just at the crucial moment. A supreme example was the late President Kennedy at his Inaugural Ceremony, as he emphasized his words with his strong Jupiterian finger pressing and pounding the table before him. Gestures of impatience with the speaker often employ both Medius and Index though all the digits may twitch under the stress of the chairman's restraint. A gentle drumming of all four fingers may indicate boredom, the difference being in the amount of energy put into the movement. Hands may be watched rubbing each other with an accent on the thumb which seems to denote working up of energy to speak out, as it is used in between the signals of the upheld hand which fails to catch the chairman's eye.

Most people can bang the table with clenched fist to underline anger; when they pound their own opposite palms one wonders whether they are reinforcing their own determination, 'taking both hands to it' or are they reprimanding themselves for some mistake?

Many speakers, especially men (which is understandable in view of women's make-up) play with their chins or faces or massage their jaw bones when in thought. This gesture appears like the genteel equivalent of scratching the head to make the brain work faster, jaw bones are so often stroked before weighty pronouncements.

Infantile Habits

Nail biting is, properly, a medical problem; frustration, infancy and kindergarten crises are naturally woven into the habit. Probably there are many causes as nails are so vulnerable to attack but with some children there seems to be a relation to mineral deficiency, on the same principle that a parrot eats its feathers when it lacks the needful fat to grow new plumage. I think that in many cases nail biting starts as in instinctive need of some dietary ingredient which has also made the nails friable; though the course of the forbidden habit may be due to other factors. Nail biting as a signal of dietary deficiency will be further considered in Chapter V, Part IV.

Thumb sucking is a return to infantilism, very often a nervous reaction, forgotten when the mind is really busy but renewed under the slightest stress of uncertainty or boredom. However that habit was considered in Chapter IV, page 62.

Babies are supposed to fold their hands with thumbs beneath the fingers in token of the Will being in abeyance. Modern babies do not seem to observe this rule; I am often astonished at the well-shaped little pink thumbs folded firmly *outside* the fingers. Continued into adult life the suppressed thumb arouses a suspicion of the proverbial 'apron strings' somewhere in the home. It is odd to see a middle-aged and apparently successful man folding his hands thus. Beware, fiancées and friends, unless there is some very strong outside history of the cause, such as a break or deformity, that man will demand a lot of mothering from his womenfolk. Women do not have as strong a tendency to hide their thumbs; when they do they will play the part of the clinging vine beautifully.

Shock

When a mind is affected by a devastatingly severe shock hands may be turned over and gazed at in a vacant, dream-like way which is a signal of dissociation of the mind; a warning of the urgent need of medical care. A Chirologist noting a change in shape or lines may also turn his hands over and peer into them, but this is done with alert intent and is not repeated over and over again.

Classical Gesture

Classical dance gestures stylize the emotions. There is a formal glossary of six positions.

Hands may be held outwards, palm up in supplication or palms downwards towards the floor in a quietening gesture.

Hands may be held with the fingers upwards with palms either outwards in arrest or defence; or towards the body in self-protection.

Hands may be held towards the side, palms towards the body in a beckoning gesture.

Arms may be raised above the head, wrists artistically curved, in joy. This last is also a frequent gesture in European folk dancing where it portrays the get-together-and-be-happy meaning illustrative of the gathering the dancers celebrate.

Indian dancers must be excepted as they have a complete language of their own. Pictures and statuettes in museums are an interesting study but only an educated Hindu dancer could explain them fully.

To consider the manual depiction of emotions in further detail : — fear is shown by the hands clasped to the body or face; horror demands elbows in, stiffened muscles, palms held towards the source of the horror in repulsion.

Anger will clench the hands and other muscles, especially the shoulders, with taut emotion.

To express love, arms are held out, palms up, the hands held a little apart though they come closer together in supplication until they suggest the whole being concentrated in the appeal. The supreme form of the supplication movement is seen in prayer when, with elbows decorously bent, fingers are brought together in an ecstasy of concentration. Of course the other conventional gesture for love is to place one or both hands over the heart area as though Cupid's darts have physically entered that organ, but this is not often genuine emotion.

At Spiritualist gatherings the hands are rested quietly on the lap, palms uppermost, in an attitude of reception. There is no need to labour these emotional gestures for they are instinctive and understood by many people of many backgrounds. There are different conventions which have to be respected; for instance in Tahiti it is very rude and unkind to wave farewell in the way we Europeans do, the gesture would mean that the departing guest is being speeded on his way. There one does a beckoning gesture inferring that one wants the guest to come back. Not everyone nods for 'Yes' and shakes the head for 'No'.

Another fascinating source of interest is to watch the power flowing from the left hand of a good conductor of an orchestra. What life that well-used hand can inspire in a performance, and how dead and automatic the music becomes without that flow of enthusiasm from the conductor. For one who is not really musical, to watch the hand, feel the response as the instrumentalists answer the summons, the gentle smoothing down, the working up of tempo and excitement to the conclusion—it is like an introduction to a new world and the key is the habit of observing hands.

PART TWO

*

DERMATOGLYPHICS

CHAPTER I

SKIN PATTERN

THIS BOOK offers an interpretation of the patterns made by the capillary ridges and furrows on fingers and palm. Some of the findings may be still at the stage of working hypotheses but all can be extensively supported by the library of prints being collected by the S.S.P.P.

A magnifying glass is essential to see the paths of the ridges. A coarse skin may be seen with the naked eye; a little talcum powder put on the finger pads or palm and lightly brushed off may help in an emergency; but magnification is indispensable for accurate work.

A print is the ideal method of working on skin patterns. There are points, technically known as 'Tri-Radii', where the lines across the base of the finger pad meet the line of ridges from the pattern. Find this little triangle and trace an ink line on the pattern from there. This ink line will bring out the pattern which encloses the core. Trace an ink line also from the centre of the core to wherever it may lead. When two or three ink lines define a pattern there is no difficulty about identification of the type nor about correct filing.

This procedure will be found equally valuable when the palmar patterns are in question as in Chapters IV and V.

These patterns are the only design on the hand which is static, unalterable as a pattern, though they are subject to the normal changes of size in growth of the hand in youth and shrinkage of old age. The pattern is formed with the formation of the skin and endures until the skin itself disintegrates. When the surface is cut so deeply as to leave a scar

Fig. 46—Print traced for analysis. Refer to page 149: dots on Heart Line, and to page 147: too fine Head Line

the join is not always perfect but the design may be followed in the same way as a geologist can follow the strata of earth when a rift has occurred. The lines match though at a different level.

Among the many thousands of hand-prints studied by Francis Galton F.R.S. (see Appendix) he only found one infinitesimal change between babyhood and boyhood—a tiny island in a ridge had joined itself up into a thickening of the ridge.

The texture or rhythm changes when the pattern breaks down through ill-health or some peculiar work, but the dots or strokes which remain follow the original pattern which returns with the restoration of health to the skin. Criminals have tried various ways of changing their finger prints but the pattern has always returned. All police systems of identification would break down if two sets were ever discovered to be identical though the differences can be very subtle, necessitating an enlargement of the prints and an exact counting of the ridges and furrows making up the shape.

The capillary ridges are formed by the thickening of the skin above and below epidermis level and contain the little openings of the sweat glands. The whole area also contains countless nerve endings. When it is remembered that specific nerves can only perform one task and that the hand is the focal point for the sense of touch, one begins to realize what a vast network the fingers and palm must contain. Nerves for heat and cold; nerves for judging weight; nerves for estimating distance to pick up objects without breaking them; nerves to control touch and grip; nerves to open and shut the sweat glands . . . their number is legion and explains the very close connection between hand and brain.

The various patterns of nerve wiring shown on fingers and palm seem to indicate how we are 'wired-up' in our brain. One hoped there would be a correlation with encephalographic readings but, so far, that avenue has not been properly explored. It is not a correlation which can be caught quickly by superficial examination.

So far work on Dermatoglyphics has been done on a strictly statistical basis—for example such-and-such a pattern occurs on the hands of ninety per cent of children with a special affliction and so on. Biologists and anthropologists acknowledge a mutual indebtedness but both sides mistrust the possibility of the patterns having any meaning, showing any facet of character of their own.

This diffidence is hardly surprising as our published information is so sparse in the West. Conte St. Germain (*Palmistry for Professional Purposes*) wrote of the apex of the skin pattern as being the true centre of a mount, but everyone seems to have ignored that fact for many years and continued to write of the fleshy eminence as being the 'displaced' mount. Vital, enduring skin pattern was not seriously studied in relation to personality and health until Noel Jaquin began his work on the break-down of the pattern as a preliminary warning of ill-health.

One correlation between hands and encephalograph readings was published in 1951. Dr. Doust of the Maudsley Hospital, London, allowed it to be known that he was working on a

Fig. 47—Patterns of blood vessels under nail

pattern of blood vessels under the nail. He found that in normal people these capillaries develop the straight-across lines of babyhood (A) into long hair-pin shape (B), normally by the age of eight years. People who are immature mentally, give way to impulse and rage, have only developed their pattern into arches (C), while neurotic people have the long form but with a twist in it (D). These findings have been checked with brain wave tests and found to correspond.

How much the Chinese knew about the persistence of skin pattern we do not know; there are examples of digital patterns on clay and other pottery but one Empress signed with the *tip* of her finger.

We of the S.S.P.P. contend that an appreciation of the attitude to life symbolized by this patterning is absolutely

ssential to understanding the personality. The design demon-
trates the 'tools' with which we have been endowed by inheri-
ance and how we have to blend the paternal and maternal
nfluences to take the best advantage from both sides.

Left Hand, Right Hand

The study of skin pattern has confirmed that the old adage
bout left hand being 'what you are born with' and right hand
what you make of it' is so superficial and incomplete as to
be nonsense. Babies are born with patterns and lines on both
hands.

Both hands can and do change shape and lines, but where
here is a divergence between the skin patterns on left and
ight hands, time after time we can describe the respective
parents as we see one mirrored on each hand. Where the
patterns are very different—a complete set of whorls on one
hand and loops on the other, for example—the outlook of
inheritance from each side may be such that the owner cannot understand himself until he realizes that he has to combine
and use the two factors which his parents found so difficult
to adjust between themselves. (See Figs. 92 and 93, pages
216-7.)

We admit that on a right-handed person the right will be
the active, day-to-day behaviour as shown to the world,
whereas the left will picture the more sub-conscious side of
dreams and memories, but in emergencies the left, the sub-
conscious or instinctive takes over control. The right will often
show how the dreams are being worked out or neglected. Also
before the onset of illness the right hand will show the break-up
of pattern and line, the left hand joins in when the ill-health
is recognized. The right hand will clear up with the physical
recovery but the left hand only follows when we have forgotten
about the illness, or ceased to talk about 'my operation'.

When interpreting skin patterns the two Index fingers, the
two Medius (Saturn) and so on should be assessed together
as one enhances or restrains the attitude to life shown by the
other. This is mentioned when consideration is being given
to each finger but this balance is of such importance that it
cannot be too strongly noted.

CHAPTER II

FINGER PAD PATTERNS

THE THREE 'worlds' symbolized by a picture of a tree, comes into the placing of the patterns on the fingers.

When the centre of the pattern is low down, in the direction of the base of the finger, near the first joint, the pattern will be expressed in some practical, physical way. High, towards the tip of the finger, the pattern will be expressed in theories, in abstract thought, in ideas if not ideals. In the centre of the phalange the message will be balanced, able to be expressed in any direction as needed by the owner.

FINGER PRINT PATTERNS

There are five basic patterns, each with its individual meaning. There are several sub-divisions and an infinite number of combinations may be found.

The basic messages of the five patterns are:

Loops, show a graceful, adaptable outlook on life. Best for team work. Sometimes symbolized as a reed.

Whorls ('fixed') the sign of the individualist. A whorled hand wants to perform or organize any task himself.

Arches ('fixed') are essentially practical people. Reliable.

Composite, this pattern is composed of entwined loops and may be summed up as a warning of a dual approach to life.

Tented arches, this pattern looks like a loop that has been frozen upright in the middle of the phalange. So have their ideas. This is the sign of the enthusiast, the reformer but they are inclined to say 'Why don't *They*?' rather than get on with the task themselves.

Francis Galton finally divided his classification into three for recording purposes—Loops, Arches and Whorls.

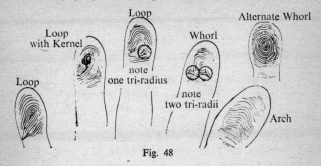

Fig. 48

Loops

The loop is the pattern most frequently found all over the world. Loops look graceful, flexible, ready to fling themselves like a lariat over any ideas they may meet. Owners of a complete, or nearly complete set will be adaptable people, good at team work, interested in new ideas. They often have the gift of being able to comfort the unhappy.

There are two types of loop, the Ulna where the lariat is thrown from the percussion side of the hand, and the Radial where the throw is from the thumb direction.

Radial loops are found most frequently on the Index finger; sometimes on the thumb, and but rarely on the other fingers. Among my records of looped Index fingers, twenty-five per cent are from the Radial direction but I have only two on third fingers among recent prints.

There is an important difference in behaviour between Radial and Ulna loops on the first finger in that the Radial ones can be adaptable, as long as the choice is from among their own interests, they must do the choosing. The Ulna loops are more inclined to act on suggestions that Fortune or other people may present to them.

A loop on the right index of a right-handed person enables him to improvise, to act in various capacities. If the loop is on the left index with a whorl or arch on the right, he will see his way round obstacles encountered by the more 'fixed' type, think of ideas for the right hand to put into operation according to its own pattern.

Loops on the second finger, nearly always Ulna, will study religious theories, have an open mind on metaphysical subjects and can talk about varying topics. When the loop is low on the finger the interest may be in forestry, farming, magistrate's work and, all the ramifications of the down-to-earth aspect of life. Loops placed high on the finger may be encountered in research teams. They all allow some flexibility of approach even though there be more static patterns on the first fingers.

Loops on third fingers, nearly always of the Ulna type, show appreciation of new ideas in fashions and in everything that conforms to the owner's idea of beauty. When the core is low on the phalange the interest is among the arts of furnishing, decoration of houses, flowers and clothes; while the higher the innermost loop the more the interest will be centred in *Art* with a most capital 'A'.

Professor Penrose, when at the Galton Laboratory, discovered that a radial loop on the third finger is associated with a disturbance of rhythm in the arrangement of the chromosomes. We have not enough examples to check the attitude to art and happiness but one of my collection is on the hands of a portrait artist.

The loop occurs on nearly ninety per cent of little fingers and is the ideal pattern for that finger as it allows the utmost response; helps in all forms of expression, complements a pointed tip of humour and aids the harmonious working of the instinctive self. I have never seen a Radial loop on the Mercury finger.

Thumbs with loops show that the will can be easily and variously expressed—if the shape of the thumb shows that there is a will to express. Where the thumbs are not strong a pair of loops trying to control a set of stronger patterned fingers finds itself being led out of the true path to follow any will-o'-the-wisp shown as a possibility by the rest of the hand. A loop on one thumb can give grace and speed to a more static patterned partner. On one thumb the loop can be helpful, but a pair must be recognized and not allowed to become too accommodating. For example—a very kind hand may express itself in various, perhaps unnecessary, actions when the rest of the digits are wanting to do some serious and essential work. Looped thumbs with whorled fingers find their most useful métier when the fingers are compelled to work with other people; the thumbs can adapt the individualistic outlook to the vagaries of committee and patrons yet keep their own objective intact.

Whorls

The *Whorl* pattern is of great importance because it has a very strong influence and is sometimes known as 'fixed'. About twenty-five per cent of all digital prints have a whorl; it is most frequently found on the third finger but may be expected on an Index or thumb. There are two forms:

Concentric circles show the whorl in its most definite form, consisting of a number of complete circles, one inside the other, with two 'tri-radii' points where the circles meet the usual straight lines across the base of the phalange. The pair of tri-radii decide whether the finger can be designated a true whorl or whether it is a loop with a kernel or whorl within it which is known to the Indians as a 'peacock's eye'. Sometimes one of the points may be so far round the finger that it does not show on a carelessly taken print. If there is any doubt the finger should be rolled separately from the whole print so that any triangles are fully shown.

The *Shell* pattern appears as though an engraver had started from the centre and drawn round and round until he reached the lines across the base. The Shell pattern carries all the usual meanings of the whorl but in a less intense degree.

The whorl is essentially the mark of the individualist.

When we discussed finger tips we quoted Dr. Benham's picture of all the ideas in the air being drawn into the mind through the fingers. To continue his fantasy imagine the ideas having to journey round all the circles before speeding on their way to the brain, and, the brain having acknowledged the reception, returning the message of action or comment by the same slow route. This allegory illustrates how deeply the personal view can imprint itself on the response of the whorled type of fingers.

D

There is often a slowness about whorled people's reactions, one cannot hurry their decisions; they require time to decide any change of view or programme. Here is a paradox because whorls can be extremely quick in an emergency. Training is so deeply absorbed that the response is instinctive and therefore fast. This may be the reason why this type of print is so often found on the hands of people who have to meet emergencies.

Whorled first fingers, which number more than a quarter of normal hands, show this individuality in their contacts with other people. They must have their own niche. If the whorl is on the right hand he will make or find the niche, but if accompanied by a loop on the left index they will have more flexibility in the choice of niche. When the order is reversed they will appear able to fulfil any role, but they will be happy only when they have made a specialized corner for themselves within that career.

On both index fingers the pattern has its strongest effect. There will be a vocational spirit so that the niche must not only be their very own, something they feel no one else could fulfil quite as well, it must also be of use to the community. As ever the height of the centre of the pattern will show the 'world' in which all these instincts will manifest. For instance, a highly placed centre might write books about the subject of its vocation while a low one will lay the foundations.

On the second finger the influence of the whorl is strong. Ideas on philosophy and planning will be self-determined and there may be a gift for original research as opinions are individualistic and not easily changed. With one of the Saturn fingers looped there may be a wider breadth of vision but the whorl will enable the owner to select the part that is important for his own work. Whorls often have a very sincere religion on far from orthodox lines.

Third fingers often have a whorled pattern even when the rest of the fingers do not share this form. The selectivity will show in the ideas of beauty and happiness. For instance, both third fingers whorled make the clothes and home of the owner intensely personal; changing art forms will not be accepted readily and fashions will have to be adapted to suit the individuality of the whorled Apollo. The owner knows his own preferences and nothing will dissuade him from them, no matter how peculiar his idea of happiness or unorthodox his approach to any art form.

A whorl on the third finger of one hand teamed with a loop on the other allows the owner to look at modern trends but the choice will still be strictly selective. This combination has proved useful to a buyer at a big London fashion house—to quote one striking example from my prints.

Whorls on the finger of Mercury are often found on a long nail phalange which should mean a good power of expression, yet they are loth to speak and prefer to be the power behind the throne. So one thinks—but let a subject arise on which the owner feels deeply and unsuspected oratory will flow. Ordinarily the whorled little finger shows painstaking sincerity in the organization of anything that is undertaken.

A difficult combination to read correctly is found when the first and second fingers are looped with the third and fourth whorled. The thumb and the rest of the hand will need even more study than usual because the character will appear adaptable, graceful and so on, yet there will be unexpected reticence and depths which can make the behaviour rather unpredictable, even to the owner.

Whorled thumbs ruling whorled fingers show a harmonious if possibly, slightly slow temperament. This pattern usually creates a very strong thumb. Instinct may suggest that once the mind is made up change will be almost impossible so decisions must be made with deliberation and care. The position of the core of the pattern is important on the thumb; placed low the owners are inclined not to bother about theories but to be decisive about material questions; while the opposite, highly placed centre, will not bother about where or how he lives but be most determined about political or theoretical questions, about books or music or plays. Easement will show if one thumb only bears the whorl with a loop on the other hand. The loop influence may be apparent in behaviour but the strength is available and ready to be roused.

For the purpose of indices and filing, distinction is made between whorls which have a tiny circle for the core and those which have a little line, but I have not found any difference in their interpretation. I have one example of a large outer circle with a grid lying along the finger pad. This is a typical form for apes where the grain runs down the fingers from nail to joint, but I have found no relation to an ape in my human example.

Arch

In the few books which mention finger pad patterns the arch is said to be atavistic, down to earth, often referred to as being low in the scale of evolution, with a reference to monkeys. Some writers have even suggested that they are the predominant type for backward tribes. Having no tri-radii they are ignored in the genetic research counts at the Galton Laboratory. In my experience this is a completely false interpretation, and I welcomed the support of Dr. Debrunner who has never met an arched finger print in his very intensive investigation of the skin patterns of the monkey and ape species.

It so happens that I have worked with a good many people who show arched patterns, especially on the Index finger. I have found them the salt of the earth. In character they remind one of the Roman bridge their patterns resemble—trustworthy, capable, when things go wrong they cope, and they have an innate courage which emphasizes their reliability.

Those attributes attain their highest expression on the Index fingers, one of the fingers arched will impart this practical capability to any loop or whorl with which it may be companioned on the other hand.

Arches on both first fingers have one serious disability which is aggravated when there are four or more arches among the ten digits, they cannot express their own thoughts or inward feelings. This peculiarity is discussed in the Chapter on the psychological effect of skin pattern on health but the reticence can be misleading. Writing or sketching can often express the feelings they cannot put into words, so that spatulate tips are a harmonious complement.

Arched second fingers demand that their religion will make people better, happier; they are rarely attracted by the ceremonial or decorative side unless it has historical or achitectural value. The same attitude is shown towards their investments, property that can be reclaimed or improved, businesses they can work up and sell all seem to attract arched digits.

Third fingers rarely have arches except as one of a complete set. When found they indicate that the artistic expression will be in something useful. As a typical example—a whorl on the left hand with an arch on the right produced prize-winning knitting.

Arches occur on fourth fingers when they are part of a complete set or part of a hand with dominant arches. When present they seem to increase the reticence and restrict artistic expression. Conversation tends to domesticity, business or other people's doings. The published records endorse the rarity of little finger arches placing the figure at one per cent (Cummins and Midlo *Finger-Prints, Palms and Soles*).

The arch is a frequent pattern on thumbs often accompanying a strong Will (nail) phalange. The owners of these thumbs do not bother with theories or abstract thought but make up their minds with efficiency on practical subjects. Arches are the ideal pattern on the thumbs of people with pointed fingers because they make the ideas of the pointed fingers materialize in constructive effort.

There is not much divergence in the high or low placing of arches on thumbs because to be an arch it is necessarily low. There is, however, a combination with a ridge or two of loop called a 'vestige' which is not unusual. If there are more than two loops the print is filed among the Loops, but in assessing character and potentialities the arch is the basic reading. The strands of loop allow an easement, a flexibility and less restricted self-expression. As an example—such a pattern on the first finger would help to find new and different ways out of a dilemma which a pure arch might not see. On the third finger the strands may allow more grace and novelty in the arrangements of house or flowers; and would be definitely helpful to the power of expression when found on the Mercury finger.

I have no satisfactory example of a minute whorl in the centre of an arch, any group of concentric circles would class the pattern as a whorl.

CHAPTER III

FINGER PRINT PATTERNS

WHILE THE division of finger print patterns into three main groups is a convenient form of official index, for a psychological study we must include at least seven of the nine groups laid down by Purkenje (see Appendix).

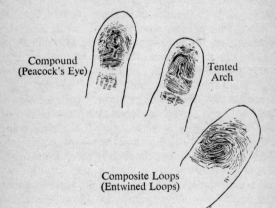

Compound
(Peacock's Eye)

Tented
Arch

Composite Loops
(Entwined Loops)

Fig. 49—Less frequent patterns

Composite

A Composite or entwined loop pattern has two tri-radii and therefore is indexed as 'Whorl', but the mental attitude is diametrically opposite. In the same way the 'Tented Arch' has nothing in common with the reliable, practical arches.

The Composite pattern is found on thumbs, index fingers, or sometimes, on the third finger. Former statistics both of Scotland Yard and Dr. Charlotte Wolff stress the rarity of this composite pattern on the second finger. I have two examples, both born since 1940, where there is a dominance of this form of print in the hands. In one pair seven out of the ten digits bear the entwined loops. So far we lack proof that this pattern is becoming more frequent but Astrologers will see the increase as heralding the Aquarian Age.

A Composite may take the form of a neat little S bend kernel to another pattern, or a large, easily recognized pair of entwined loops. When traced with an ink line they may leave the finger pad on opposite sides. Wherever this pattern is located it warns of the divided thoughts about the finger or palmar area beneath. One Fellow of the S.S.P.P. declares the entwined loops are reminiscent of the song about the 'Right-handed honeysuckle to Left-handed Columbine' whose offspring fell flat on their faces. The duality of thought as exemplified by the loops without the clarity of whorl or loop alone, creates confusion of thought. The strength of the pattern lies in the ability to see both sides of any position. The weakness lies in the difficulty of choosing between them leading, at times, to an inner conflict and self-mistrust.

On the Jupiter finger composite patterns are very useful on the hands of a lawyer, an administrator, anyone who has to see both sides of a problem. They often get into trouble at school for quickly seeing the opposite of any statement a teacher may make, so they are accused of being argumentative. When one has to work with the owner of composite patterned index fingers the easiest way is to put a question and let the loops work out the answer themselves. Recognized and controlled, a large, definite pattern can be a helpful gift on a first finger. When the design is small, hardly noticeable at first glance, one often finds a little reservation in their responses, questioning of their own ideas, but not the direct argument as with a true entwined loop pattern.

The rarity of occurrence on a second finger precludes any definite statement. There is one interpretation of the entwined loops; that they show conflict between spiritual and material values. This might be a suitable explanation when found on the Medius finger which is so closely associated with the ethical aspect of religion.

Third fingers can have the composite sign but less often than thumb and index. I first met it on the hands of a judge at important dog shows who had a name for very great care, for independence of opinion, but also for being irritatingly slow. This weighing of values might be associated with the ability to see too many facets of choice.

Have people with composite prints on their 'Beauty and Happiness' fingers more than ordinary difficulty in deciding their idea of the beautiful? Are they more inclined than other patterns to support the revolt of the new art forms?

When in company with a very decisive, conscious side of the hand, i.e. index and thumb with whorls or arches, probably no difference will be shown in their artistic appreciation. They may defend ardently either the new or the antique. The dual effect may be found in their emotional life, in the happiness aspect of the third finger. It must be remembered that the third finger holds the combination of aesthetic appreciation and the emotional response which is necessary for true happiness—standards of the aesthetic appreciation remaining strictly personal.

Composite pattern on the thumb. When a 'Handbook of Hands' appeared people with this pattern on their thumbs were asked to communicate with the author. We had many prints, and with no exception the owners admitted to experiencing much difficulty over making up their minds to a specific course of action. They did things, said things, and regretted them later. When I see this design now I beg the owner to sleep on a problem, decide quickly when waking, then stick to the decision, warning him or herself of all the things that could have gone *wrong* had that decision not been taken. Should this composite patterned thumb be accompanied by a Girdle of Venus which enables the owner to envisage the delights of the rejected path, the position has the ingredients of much unhappiness, but this argument is for Chapter II, Part III, page 155.

A loop on one thumb helps decisions to be made more

quickly and only questioned later. On an otherwise good, courageous hand the one composite can make the owner look all round a problem and make the best of his decision.

With a whorled companion the composite can increase the delays of the whorl and be difficult to get started on anything.

An arch seems a rare partner but one can imagine the opposing thumbs becoming very much annoyed with each other.

The composite pattern on first fingers is a responsibility which may be used constructively; on thumbs it can constitute a serious problem postulating lessons to be learnt.

Tented Arch

The sixth basic pattern is the tented arch. Imagine a loop which, finding itself straight up the middle of a finger pad supported by a single tent pole or a stiff narrow loop core, there froze. The design is a very exact symbol of the attitude of mind this figure represents. The grace and flexibility of the loop are stiffened into rigidity.

Tented arches appear most frequently on Index fingers; I have only one print of a thumb thus patterned, and I have no full set. Four examples among the ten digits are a high count. I am told that the percentage is higher among apes, possibly because the natural direction of papillary ridges on anthropoid hands is aligned with the fingers. I do not know whether apes have the capacity displayed by the human wearers of the pattern.

When present on the first finger enthusiasm is most marked, usually for a 'Cause'. But the owners do put drive into movements and are invaluable at getting anything started. How enduring the current enthusiasm will be must be judged from the degree of flexibility of the thumbs, a stiff thumb will keep the pot simmering for a long time while a very flexible thumb will allow the effort to be transient, with the interest returning from time to time to keep the movement whipped up—in the usual cycle of flexible thumbs. It will be remembered that a good flexible thumb can allow the owner to return again and again to his former works; the advantage lies in the fresh viewpoint. When allied with tented arch first fingers there is a danger of their being a little overwhelming to their colleagues.

The few second fingers I have met with tented arches have been even more followers of 'isms' than when the enthusiasm is applied by the personal finger. Two converts to Communism and one to a change of religion have led me to expect this 'ism' explanation, but I have not one-tenth of the hundred examples demanded by true enquiry.

When it is found on the third finger several writers associate the pattern with a gift for music, but there does not seem to be any definite proof as yet. With all the time and hard work the study of music involves this insignia would appear to be ideally placed.

With only one example of a tented arch appearing on a Mercury finger I do not feel one can suggest any attribute. There is much more work to be done, more examples to be found before its special character can be isolated. However, if the first finger is also tented the two, the conscious and subconscious sides of the temperament, would work harmoniously together.

Compound Patterns

The effect of a few strands of loop within an arch was noted in the preceding chapter. There is also a large class of pattern showing some concentric circles of a whorl within a loop. This is one of the patterns recognized by Purkenje. Sometimes it takes the form of a perfect eye in a peacock's tail feather. When a nicely formed core is found within a loop the owner seems to combine the charm of the loop with the gift of discernment or selection. Sometimes the pattern seems to take the shape of the actual form of a human eye, when one is not being fanciful to expect a high degree of the power of observation.

Indian tradition sees in a peacock's eye on the third finger a promise of protection in physical danger. One Fellow of the S.S.P.P. quotes four prints out of eighty on the hands of not particularly lucky people but each had survived tragedy. From my own files I can endorse that so far everyone I have asked, with this third finger pattern, has agreed that there has been much luck in dangerous situations.

Any of the patterns may be combined in an adaptation peculiar to one example. It would be impossible to lay down laws or suggest hypotheses for all of them. Therefore first study the fingers with clear patterns, then return to the difficult one, remembering the inherent possibilities of any ridge form present, and see in the blending of them the attitude to life as assessed by that digit.

Sometimes in the uncertainty of the finger pattern one can find the conflict which has led the owner to seek the help of hand interpretation.

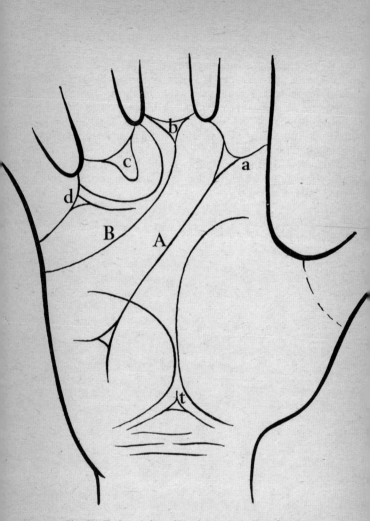

Fig. 50—To locate the radii and trace main line of pattern

CHAPTER IV

APICES

THIS CHAPTER will be much more easy to follow if the hand-print recommended in a previous chapter (page 90) is used again.

In an ink which shows up well on a black print, mark the tri-radius points to be found under the fingers and in the palm. These points will bear the reference in small lettering. Trace the direction of the three lines forming the tri-radius.

The main ridge away from the fingers, towards the palm will have the same letter as the tri-radius from whence it started but written in capital letters.

The apices below the heart line are known as 'axial' with the nearest one to the wrist 'proximal' labelled 't'.

This is the scientific usage which is not difficult to follow and a useful habit should one want to check the frequency of occurrence of a pattern or convert co-workers to a facet of our interpretation.

When we consider the skin pattern on the palm we are confronted by an anomaly.

The word 'apex' infers a top or summit so that one would expect to find the tri-radii on the highest point of the fleshy eminences under the fingers. Yet, since St. Germain's book *Palmistry for Professional Purposes*, we have recognized the apex of these mounts at the tri-radii in the troughs between the pads.

As we saw in Chapter III the three central fleshy eminences or mounts at the top of the palm have to lie between the digits if they are to do their work of protecting the dividing nerves

ing nerves and blood vessels to a safe journey up the sides of the fingers; while directly in front of a finger the trough shows the path of the tendon.

I suggest, therefore, that we view the mounts themselves as power producers or condensers for the energy available to the instinctive thoughts inherent in the finger, and the tri-radii beneath each finger as a switch or key directing the course of the energy. The triangle then becomes the summit or apex of the power.

There are several different forms of the meeting of the lines. Indian tradition sees great value in the differences, but this part of the skin pattern seems to be yet more sacred than the finger prints. So far the S.S.P.P. has only found a hypothesis for the elongated loop form (Fig. 51, X, page 113) under the third finger. Y and Z have no separate meaning as yet.

The apex should be found directly beneath the centre line of Index, Medius and Ring finger but aligned with the inner side of the little finger. The study of the position of these apices is essential to good hand-interpretation but clearly understood that they denote tendencies, instinctive ways of thought and behaviour, which can be hidden by strong thumbs or conflicting lines. The habitual attitude to life which these skin pattern marks portray may be hidden but must never be underrated.

Apices follow the 'Tree' symbol in their position. When they are close to the finger, i.e. not more than six or seven ridges from the line of attachment, they may be classed as high. At about fourteen ridges and over they are classed as low; but the Saturn mount habitually has the apex higher than the two boundary fingers of Jupiter and Mercury. Apollo is very variable.

Apices may deviate out of true centre. The medial position seems to encourage the finger to be held straight while there is often a tendency for the tip of a finger to lean over when the apex of the mount is not true centre of the finger. The divergence of fingers from the straight, especially in young hands, can respond to environmental influences. As a practical example, a scientist with the triangle very high may work from a love of abstract thought, of seeking just a little further into

the unknown, or with a low one of fifteen to seventeen ridges
he may be motivated by a longing to serve humanity. The
motive of his working life will be shown by the height or depth
or placement of the apex of his Jupiter mount.

Mount of Jupiter

The tri-radii of Jupiter (Fig. 50, a) seems one of the most
important signs for the estimation of character and probable
behaviour. Aligned with the centre of the finger it is the mark
of personal integrity. With this placement on both hands the
owner has to keep his own self-respect. He may be a gambler
or even a burglar but he will not do anything mean, anything
of which he, from the point of view of a gambler or one brought
up to the burglaring business, would consider mean.

Out of place towards the second finger the manifestation of
Self in relation to other people is directed to practical ends;
often the weight of responsibility as the mother of a family or
the foreman or shop-steward in a factory. In sum the deviation
is towards the 'background' of life inherent in the Saturnian
finger.

When out of place, towards the thumb side of the hand,
the apex warns of a sense of irresponsibility. The attitude can
be tamed into a love of adventure and may be found, often on
one hand only, among pioneers or descendants of such adventurous folk. This radial deviation seems to be of frequent
occurrence on American hands and, to quote from prints and
sketches, I have met with it on New Zealanders.

Highly placed, close to the finger line, the apex will demon-
strate a leaning towards the intelligent or intellectual approach
and may have the danger of a rather egotistical outlook. Low,
towards the life line, the expression will be on a practical plane
so that central and lower placing produces the idea of service.
Strong Jupiterian leadership can find happy expression in our
British habit of voluntary service.

Mount of Saturn (Fig. 50, b)

The apex of this mount is always higher than the others so
its relative position must be counted on a lower number of
skin ridges.

Centrally placed it suggests a sound judgement about property and values. On spendthrift hands it seems to edge off towards the third finger. Not all people who have the apex out of place towards Apollo are extravagant, but people who are ill-advised about finance seem to have the apex displaced I have never seen one displaced towards the first finger.

The proximity to the finger line follows the usual rule, very close one expects good theoretical judgement whereas when the triangle is further away the interest is more likely to be in real estate or farming. Sometimes the apex of the mount is not in harmony with the placing of the finger print, the apex may be set very high while the patterns on the finger are set low or vice versa. Here, I think, the answer is to examine both hands: if there are three low positions to one high then the high indication is probably inherited from a parent or grandparent who had very sound or theoretical skill which may be dormant, but ready to appear again in the next generation. Both apices high and both finger patterns low have been seen on the hands of a maker of intricate models, also of a consulting engineer where his work took him out to the sites.

Sometimes, when the apex retreats towards the third fingers the tip of the finger is drawn in that direction as well, so that the palmar pattern is responsible for the duty versus happiness conflict we studied in Chapter III, Part I, (page 50).

When the Saturnian apex is linked in the skin ridges with the apices of Apollo or Mercury, astrologers seek some connection in the position of the Planets in the natal chart. For palmists the link seems to induce a combination of the two aspects, the writer or speaker who has a definite purpose in his work or the artistic creation used in some constructive way.

Mount of Apollo (Fig. 50, c)

The third apex is frequently drawn towards the radial side of the hand but more rarely outwards except when the triradii are duplicated as when a loop enters the hand between the fingers. This loop has a meaning of its own but does not seem to affect or give special meaning to the apex.

Sometimes the tri-radii point itself is difficult to find when there is a formation of ridges beneath the finger, looking rather like a 'Giraffe woman's' collar. When this collar lies deep in the palm it seems to cut off spontaneous enjoyment. The 'life and soul' of the party never has this collar, unless he is a professional humorist with the streak of sadness that makes the true clown. It is important that people with this form pause when they are enjoying anything, be it the beauty of a sunset or the rhythm of a dance, pause and register their happiness with their conscious minds. If they learn the habit they will

Fig. 51—Varieties of tri-radii

grow 'Sun' lines across the graining of the skin and conquer a pattern which might be considered a handicap (Fig. 92, page 216).

A central, high or fairly high apex is of great help to an artist in any branch of creative expression.

The triangle of papillary ridges under the third finger can take the form of a loop towards the heart line (Fig. 51, X).

A Fellow of the S.S.P.P. noticed a large proportion on the hands of Members of a Pony Club. She made further search and finally postulated that this form of tri-radius went with a love of animals. This meaning has since been borne out by inquiries among other Members. On one hand only there can be an inheritance with a story of a parent, aunt or grandparent who is especially devoted and skilled with animals. On both hands the interpretation of the loop seems infallible; the longer the loop extends the greater the devotion.

When the apex lies in the direction of the second finger and the tip leans over it one finds the psychological complexities of the two middle fingers out of alignment have been enhanced.

Mount of Mercury Fig. 50, d)

While the normal position of the fourth apex is in line with the inside edge of the finger it is sometimes found directly underneath as with the other three. The farther it lies towards the central position the greater the love and appreciation of words. Not necessarily the music of words as in poetry, but as living instruments with history and meaning and subtleties of their own. Sir Winston Churchill is reputed to have had central apices under his little fingers and, at the other end of the scale, one owner has expressed a passion for crossword puzzles.

The ideal height for this apex is level with that of the first finger when there will be inner harmony between the two sides of the personality.

Mount of Venus

Apices may also appear on the Mount of Venus (Thenar Eminence). On many British hands they are difficult to locate and when there is an arch-like swerve there is no more a true tri-radius than there is on an arched finger print. On many Oriental hands there is a definite and easily definable central point, and I have found such a point strongly marked on hands with Jewish blood, but have not enough evidence to suggest any rule.

In the measurement of time recommended by Cheiro, this point on the thumb is the base of the radial lines he drew to the finger mounts to divide the life into periods. The difficulty in finding this point as a base is probably the reason that the method is not always successful, but where there is a good clear mark on the print the timing laid down by Cheiro can be accurate.

Mount of Neptune (Fig. 50, t)

There can be a triangle type apex in the very centre of the wrist boundary of the palm. This will be found of importance when we study the line of 'Fate'. I think the pattern may focus the centre of an eminence which I regard as the 'earth' connection of the Pineal Gland. When thus accentuated there is a possibility of 'awareness', some practical form of E.S.P. This is another of the apices which may correlate with Astrology.

Tri-radii points are also found about one half to five-eighths of the way from the wrist boundary in the direction of the third finger on the percussion side of the 'Plain of Mars'. Biologists are building up evidence of correlation between the mark and pre-natal heart conditions. For Palmists the placing responds to a memory of sensation, of how things *felt* both emotionally and in texture. This reading is only a hypothesis but supported by writers who can remember their feelings sufficiently vividly to reproduce them on demand; and when one asks an owner about this gift of memory the interpretation is accepted, often with a little story of a childhood experience.

This apex may accompany patterns on the Hypothenar Eminence which are to be discussed in the next chapter.

Mount of Luna (Hypothenar Eminence)

Indian practitioners have told me that an apex on the lower part of the Mount of Luna, (Fig. 59, page 133), with a line through or from the centre, indicates that success will never be recognized. They call the mark the sign of the worker for other people to reap the harvest. I have the sign on both hands and have found the interpretation all too true.

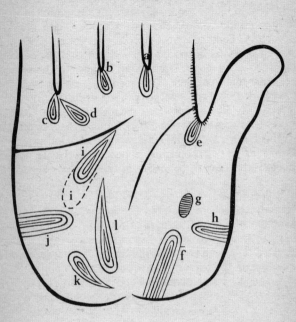

Fig. 52—Palmar patterns: *Interdigital*:   a: Rajah
                                           b: Serious Intent
                                           c: Humour
                                           d: Vanity
                                         e: Courage
                      Thenar: f: Music
                                         g: 'Bee' (strings)
                                         h: Brass Music
        Hypothenar: i: Memory
                                         j: Nature (Ulna)
                                         k: Inspiration
        Parathenar: l: Humanism

CHAPTER V

PALMAR PATTERNS

FOLLOWING THE design of the last chapter we will start with the patterns on or between the mounts beneath the fingers (Fig. 52).

Rajah (Fig. 52, a)

A loop entering the palm between the first and second fingers does occur from time to time. In 1957 I checked two hundred pairs of prints and found twelve examples, since then they have appeared on about six per cent of hand prints, with which figure Dr. Debrunner concurs. A Palmist friend in Nairobi, who has a pair of his own, told me that in Indian tradition this loop is known as the sign of a Rajah and is supposed to show Royal blood. A Fellow of the S.S.P.P. found five examples out of eighty prints, and as four of the owners were Scottish and claim Royal descent, this meaning is supported. All but two of my prints are on the hands of people of importance in their own worlds; of the remaining two, one has kept dignity and position against very heavy adverse circumstances, while the other, delayed by a composite thumb print and other signs, may yet make good. He has personal magnetism which was an attribute strongly noted among the Scottish examples.

On the right hand alone the Rajah loops seem to operate in an executive way; on the left, one example is a young married woman with no personal ambition, however she does much entertaining in connection with her husband's position, which she enjoys and accomplishes with charm and skill.

Serious Intent (Fig. 52, b)

Loops entering the palm between the second and third fingers are of frequent occurrence. They have been defined as showing special 'sensitivity', but we find that they denote

a serious purpose in life and have named them the 'Loop of
serious intent'. On one hand only they seem to be content with
a serious hobby, but on both hands the owner will want to do
more. These loops can be found on up to fifty per cent of the
hands in gatherings of councillors and religious groups. The
graining seems to unite the happiness of the third finger with
the stability of the second so that they choose hobbies, activities and work which they feel are of service to the communal
life. They do not like to fritter away their time.

Loop of Humour (Fig. 52, c)

Between third and fourth fingers a little loop entering the
hand is an infallible sign of people with a sense of the ridiculous, people who can see the humorous side of things and
giggle from the tummy, as opposed to the mental wit shown
by a pointed Mercury finger. With loops on both hands the
owner is often accused of facetiousness, but how helpful to
the enjoyment of life when people can keep their sense of the
ridiculous even against themselves.

Sometimes the loop of humour goes astray and crosses in
front of the third finger (Fig. 52, d). I have, reluctantly, come
to the conclusion that their sense of the ridiculous is out of
focus, too, and become warped by vanity. Few owners will
recognize this trait in themselves but the deviation is a warning
to tread warily and not allow any suggestion of laughter *at* but
only *with* the distorted loop.

The loop of humour is a fairy godmother's saving gift to a
'Giraffe collar' under and around the third finger.

Without actually working out the statistical evidence, often,
when there is a third finger elongated apex on one hand there
is the loop of humour on the other. The combination seems to
work well on the basis of personality and may explain another
meaning ascribed to this form of apex—that it shows a sixth
sense or gift of understanding. An extra sense of awareness
is certainly necessary when training animals.

Any patterns other than loops are very rare under the fingers
of human hands. Whorls are typical of gorillas and other
simian hands and feet while Dr. Praechter Ben Aris of Tel
Aviv, who has done a great deal of work on police archives,

has found the hands of criminals very heavily patterned.

In our collections we have few whorls. I have only three hands with tiny circles between the third and fourth fingers. They are all a very long way from any sub-human species! I think, however, that they do lack a spontaneous sense of the ridiculous—a little slow to recognize a 'leg-pull', and apt to take an accident as an insult until a little time has elapsed, and they have been able to think things over. But what are three examples among many hundreds of prints?

Loop of Courage (Fig. 52, e)

Scientific books mention patterns between thumb and forefinger as in the first interdigital space. These patterns seem to be so psychologically attuned to our Mount of Mars beneath the life line that we will consider them in relation to the recognized attribute of Mars, courage.

Sometimes a small, neat loop enters the ball of the thumb from the Mount of Mars and points to a peculiar awareness of physical courage. There may be a worship of courage, a longing to be braver than the mount itself suggests, a frequent effort to prove that fear can be overcome. A long, rather thin attenuated form, accompanying the line of the Family ring around the joint of the thumb, pictured a long, hard fight against many difficulties waged *for the family*, which had been successful owing to the courage shown. Other members have examples in their files where the owners are outstandingly brave.

There seems to be no law that a loop on Mars must accompany a pattern lower on the Thenar Eminence but they can often be seen together. A very good example of the single type was on the hands of a Tristan da Cunha wife, mother of several children. Her husband said that he had never known her to show fear.

Thenar Eminence (Mount of Venus)

All too often a pattern on the Mount of Venus is dismissed as evidence of uninhibited sex, or at best, a passionate nature. Mothers are warned to be extra careful of their children with frowns and head-shakings. Mrs. Robinson's classic *The Graven*

Palm may be mentioned as a reference for lines at the base of the thumb, and there the inquiry is left.

Taking the mount to mean simply and basically a gauge of the capacity to feel alive, the rest of the hand should be studied to see how this gift of life is likely to be used.

Arch

The usual pattern on the ball of the thumb is the arch with the base towards the thumb and the balustrade or the bridge towards the palm; or developing from the sweep of the papillary ridges near the life line.

This may denote a practical approach so that feeling surging life may lead to throwing the lady into the Jaguar, or wheedling the mink coat or wedding ring, but the arch does represent a field still open to investigation. Arches hardly count as a real pattern on this mount, unless they are very clearly marked, because they lack radius or, indeed, any clear focus on so many Western hands.

Loop

True patterns carry a clear meaning. Where there is a definite loop rising from the border with the wrist and lying up the mount (Fig. 52, f) there will be a love of music. Not necessarily any ability to play or compose, but the owner will be tremendously moved emotionally by music. Should there be cross patterning rather like an insect bee, the response may well be felt most strongly to stringed instruments (Fig. 52, g).

We have examples of a loop entering the mount from the angle of *Time* (Fig. 52, h). In each case the response is to brass and martial music, the swing of rhythm being paramount.

A loop with the roots from the Mount of Neptune is more rare so one cannot dogmatize. Logically, with the root on the area which can express healing or magnetic power and the direction indicating a response to music, the pattern ought to coincide with the music of poetry or the music of the spheres but nature is not always logical.

I have not met with a whorl on the thenar area but the nearest to that pattern is the peacock's feather with the eye, a signal of success.

Hypo-Thenar Eminence (Mount of Luna)

This area of the hand is so frequently patterned that the title 'finger of the sub-conscious' has an element of truth as well as being a convenient memory symbol.

Patterns on the percussion have been extensively studied by biologists and anthropologists and some of their findings will be specifically mentioned in Chapter III, Part IV, but many of their comments must be included in any consideration of this part of the hand.

The most frequent type of loop (Fig. 52, i), about forty per cent, starts somewhere on the Mount of Jupiter or below near the head line, and may flow either to Luna itself, about two-thirds of the way to the wrist, or higher up, about mid-palm, so that one has to consider whether the apex of the loop is on Luna or Mars Negative.

Both the formations seem to endow their owners with an extra allowance of memory; not always the exact, active memory for use in the office but the sort that, flowering in the bath or other relaxed moments, can bring past knowledge or experience to illuminate problems. The wiring seems to take the stored awareness to the conscious mind so that, for instance, dowsers who have this sort of loop are sure their gift is psychic, from within. The description defies exact definition but watching the effect for the lucky owner one recognizes the gift.

One example of the straighter line of loop was seen on the hands of an R.A.F. pilot. He began his radial loop just above the life line, just 'North' of the mount of Mars Positive and the path lay across the hand to the percussion sloping very slightly towards the wrist. He said he had always 'felt' hostile aircraft and he knew when something was not quite right with the plane before any gauges warned. This pilot also had a very sensitive hand, so one could not prove that the loop on his percussion was responsible, but the reading has been endorsed, if in less dramatic ways.

There is a loop (Fig. 52, j), entering the hand from the Ulna side which is not as frequent, probably only on about eight per cent of all hands. The actual loop varies a little in the exact position but the interpretation remains as an awareness of outside influences especially of radiations and feelings for Mother Earth. Dowsers with this form of the pattern say that they feel an emanation from the substance they seek be it water, oil, metal or a person. The green fingers of a gardener are the fruit of this sensitivity.

'Dr. Debrunner has found this incoming pattern on ninety per cent of mongoloid (mentally afflicted) people, forty-five per cent of whom have the sign on both hands. He and the anthropologists find the mark on only about six per cent of ordinary people but I am inclined to put the proportion higher, perhaps because I have many prints of people with these unusual gifts. Among thirty-nine children born during 1945, 1946 and 1947 there were six examples, and in a collection of 300 prints there are forty-two examples of which twenty have the loop on both hands. Of these twelve have a gift of awareness and dowsing, eight are enthusiastic gardeners, while the rest either have not noticed any gift themselves or are unknown to the collectors of the prints. None show any sign of Mongolism, a living example in Fig. 86, page 184.

This does *not* mean that normal hands with the Ulna Loop show mongoloid tendencies, but there might be a pointer towards the 'Gift with the bees', or other natural forms, with which the old-fashioned village idiot was endowed. Even today these poor children act, live and survive more by instinct than by the work of their brains and frequently find their greatest happiness in their love of nature.

A loop (Fig. 52, k) may take the direction from the very centre of the base of the hand, from the Mount of Neptune. I have reason to think that the powers of imagination are being linked with the intuitive gifts of a lively, active Pineal gland. One lady with this design composes music and says that she hears it from outside herself. Another print, the hand of an engineer, said that ideas 'come to him'. We wonder whether poor, deaf Beethoven had this loop? It is such a rare sign that the quantity demanded by scientific accuracy is difficult to come by. There is an even rarer loop (Fig. 52, l) which almost follows the life line to have the looped end on or just by the Mount of Neptune from roots under the first or second fingers.

There is an Indian interpretation, but I do not know it so have had to work out a hypothesis which I cannot claim as a law, or even be sure that it is a tendency, but only a theory worth investigation.

When an imaginative head line follows the general direction of the life line towards the thumb the imagination will be focused on people, and an author writes romances synonymous with the more sentimental women's magazines. In the three examples I have of this skin pattern loop, one is a very successful young insurance agent whose kindly understanding has resulted in rapid promotion; another a palmist, so that the humanitarian aspect might be sought in this design.

Whorl (Fig. 53)

The Mount of Luna has other finger-type patterns than the adaptable loop which allows the Lunarian gifts to be borrowed by other mounts. A whorl on the hypothenar eminence keeps its individualistic characteristics and may be seen as individualizing the sub-conscious. At one end of the scale Dr. Debrunner finds the whorl on the hands of many of his schizophrenic patients. Not all whorled Luna hands belong to schizophrenics, part way along the scale is the actor who utterly identifies himself with his role; or there may be vague longings to achieve some end felt as an objective in life but not identified.

Fig. 53—Whorl on Hypothenar

As in finger whorls, the Luna edition is best used by a strong, compulsive thumb. With many looped companions the whorl can find expression in their enthusiasms, but it is one of the signs which should be regarded as a gift to be used and not an attribute to be wasted or ignored.

Composite (Fig. 54)

The Composite or entwined loop pattern is much more difficult to help. Among the thirty-nine pairs of schoolchildren

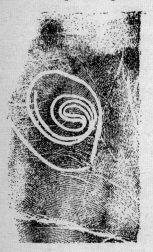

prints contributed to the library by a schoolteacher Fellow, there was only one example of a composite pattern on Luna.

There is the same duality with this form that has been found to bedevil thumbs. The owners know they want to express something, have some gift, yet whatever they start they question themselves out of performing. This duality is one of the vital signs where recognition by hand interpretation can help

Fig. 54—Composite on Hypothenar

beyond all reckoning. Once a person understands the insistent, nagging wobble at the back of his mind he or she can use it to follow the routine of looking at all sides of a problem, sleeping on it, choosing, and only looking at the gloomy side of what might have been. These patterns on the hypothenar I regard as of very great importance in psychiatric work for once the idea behind them is accepted they present a wonderful understanding of man. Fig. 55 is a rare example of a tented arch on the mount of Luna. The reading of enthusiasm and initiative certainly holds good with the owner of this hand.

According to his secretary, the enthusiasm is instinctive and vital.

Open Field (Fig. 46)

Where there is no pattern the graining flows smoothly off the percussion and is known technically as an 'Open Field'. Many country bred people have this formation. Uncluttered by introspection, using both sides of themselves in harmony with Nature, when they are angry, worried, in love or happy they can put themselves into the emotion wholly and without discord within. The lines may show frustrating emotions but it is unlikely that their own sub-conscious side will be the cause of the trouble except, possibly, by lack of understanding.

As the Open Field ridges pass under the third finger area they may open into an onion shape thus making the graining much finer. No work has been done as yet on the effect of personality of this transition.

Fig. 55—Tented arch on Hypothenar

PART THREE

*

CHIROMANCY

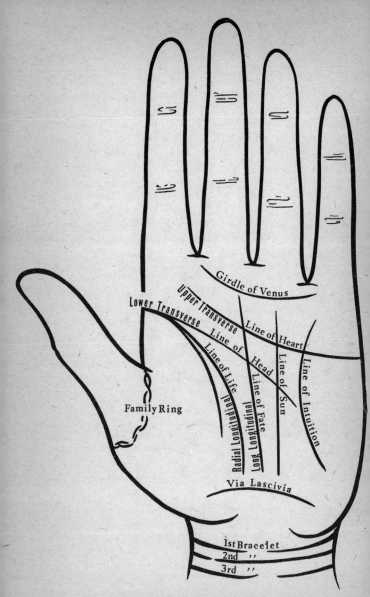

Fig. 56—Traditional and anatomical names

CHAPTER I

FLEXURE LINES

THE STUDY of the lines of the palm is the most usual form of palmistry and apt to take an undue share of the interest of an inquirer.

Books on anatomy call them 'Flexure lines' and suggest they are simply the folding of the flesh of the palm. (One can have an amusing few minutes challenging such a statement by asking for a demonstration of the movements causing, for instance, a star!)

The truth is that the flesh of the hand folds where the lines have made suitable paths.

Lines show the habitual path of thought and change in direction and texture with any stabilized variation in the habitual path of the owner's way of thinking. Therefore the immediate present attitude of mind, memories of the past and hopes for the future, may be read, but the actual future itself, with a few exceptional conditions, is unpredictable.

Exceptions take us into deep water. Some people seem to have come into this life to pursue some definite aim, learn some lesson, or suffer an experience. There is a type of hand which may well give an indication of the aim, lesson or experience and will not alter much in direction over the years. Even when such stations in life are clearly defined there is still freedom to adjust one's attitude to them; life is rarely a railway line, one can travel by devious routes as long as one calls at the destined stopping places.

The hypothesis that lines on the hand are closely related to nerve endings received dramatic support in the case of a painter

E

who fell from a height and was taken into the hospital where members of the Chirological Society were studying health on hands. The man was concussed and deeply unconscious and every line on his palms had been wiped out. As the days went on and he gradually regained consciousness the lines returned. This sudden, total extinction is rare but has been confirmed from Germany and other countries. Fading lines will be further discussed in the following chapters.

What then causes lines to appear on hands and feet?

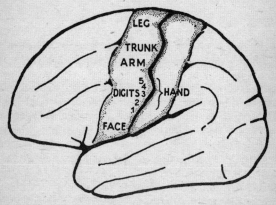

Fig. 57—Diagram of the left side of the brain to show in broad outline the situation of the cortical areas around the Fissure of Rolando. (Wood Jones: *The Principles of Anatomy as seen in the Hand*, Baillière, Tindall & Cassell.)

We know that the hand is covered with thousands of fine nerves which find their cortical termination in the nerve cells in the central sulcis or Fissure of Rolando which divides the brain like a walnut. Surgeons have proved that the hand has the lion's share of the areas devoted to both movement and to sensation.

Latest discoveries suggest that all messages to the intelligence arrive via the spinal column and its ramifications to the brain; those which require our knowledge, memory, acceptance, considered action, etc., go forward to the front part of the brain or 'dark area' as it used to be called, thus crossing the area of the terminals of nerves to the hand.

All such messages are basically electrical impulses. As an 'amateur' of electricity I know that if you hold a bunch of wire terminals and run a current across them even without actually touching you will induce a responsive current in those wires. This idea has been used extensively in the transistor sets used in America for 'snooping' as quoted in *The Reader's Digest* for September 1964. Another device is also described where the electricity of a human entering a room is sufficient to switch on an instrument: which confirms the presence of electrical power in the body.

My hypothesis, therefore, is that as we think in our brains so do the nerves send their tiny impulse to the hand, but they must be excited frequently or dramatically to show and retain the habitual path of thought on the palm.

We will be studying the changing of lines in the following chapters but we must start with the certainty that they do change and do so in both hands. At one time palmists thought that memory lines were static but a dramatic example proved that our attitude to memories can change the lines as well.

A lady who was mildly interested in hands was ill and threatened with a painful and vital disease. She kindly allowed me to take her prints at monthly intervals as she underwent treatment. Rising from her life line on to the Mount of Jupiter was a long clear island which started about the date of her marriage. As the months went on the danger was averted until one month the island had joined into one clean, strong 'effort' line. I was told I had not taken the prints properly and the colleague who was working with me took another print himself. This showed my version to be correct. Then I asked the lady what she had felt about her marriage when she was so ill? She replied that the worst part of it was her impatience with her son and daughter and her loathing of the house chores. The delight of feeling better was that she realized again that she had the best husband any woman could have, the nicest home and the young people only made happy noises as any young people should do.

Since then we have found other changes in the attitude to memories pictured on the hand.

With a right-handed person the right hand will change more

Fig. 58—1948. Note also lack of sleep. Lines change, left hands as well as right

Fig. 59—12 years later. Note apex on Luna, page 115

quickly but the left hand follows as the mind registers the alteration. With left-handed people we think the reverse holds good but there is much more work to be done on left-handedness.

Professor Wood Jones, in his *Principles of Anatomy as Seen in the Hand** states with reference to the appearances of lines in the embryo:

> They develop early, soon after the fingers, and appear upon the palm before this is the site of any active movement. In the individual they are therefore not caused by actual movements of the joints of the developing hand, but are developed as a heritage which may be used and modified by the individual. . . .

By the eighth week they may be distinguished: Life Line first, then Heart Line, with Head Line following.

Any X-ray photograph will show the notion to be at fault that declares these creases to be caused by the folding of the joints (Fig. 60). Some Heart Lines and a 'simian' line might be the 'surface registration of the mobility of parts' and mark the site of what may be termed the skin joint, brought into action by the movement of the underlying bony joint. But the theory of a permanent anchorage breaks down with the Head Line which should, and often does, lie directly across all the metacarpal bones. Though it creases as a subsidiary fold to the Heart Line in some hands, its place and direction are distinctively individual. The Life Line might be the result of using the thumb muscles, or an anchorage provided for the skin during their use, but the line may lie right across the palm away from the thumb, there may be two lines, and the Life Line is one that shows frequent and facile alterations.

Neither do flexure lines come from the way the hand is used. Craftsmen using the same tools grow hardenings and callouses in the same areas but directly the skin returns to normal the lines show independent personality. On the other side we shall see when studying the Head Line that people chosen by one person to work as a team may easily show the same type and quality of Head Line. That is discussed in detail in Chapter II, Part III.

* Baillière, Tindall & Cassell, London (Second Edition 1946).

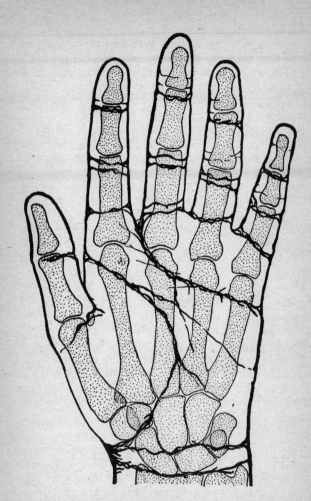

Fig. 60—The relation of the palmar lines to the bony elements of the
hand. Case of T.P. The fingers are short, and the medial digital crease is
situated nearer to the base of the finger than the medial interphalangeal
joint. Reconstructed from X-ray plates. (Wood Jones: *The Principles of
Anatomy as seen in the Hand*, Baillière, Tindall & Cassell.)

Babies used to arrive showing the mother's general pattern, but, according to the old books, with only the three main lines. Various very new babies I have seen of late years show far more than the three, some have quite clear Fate Lines and other variations. The temperament they have inherited may show, especially in the juxtaposition of Head and Life Lines under the first finger, but that peculiarity is of genetic and parental interest and not a rule.

Lines should be clear, of a colour suitable for the skin of the palm. European hands should have slightly more pinkish lines, brown backed hands have pink palms with brown lines, while the olive hand has its own shade of mushroom.

Lines should have depth and strength suitable to the weight of the palm, and free from distortions, breaks, islands and fraying. This ideal is not often achieved.

When the lines are narrow and deeply chiselled there will be a brittleness about the temperament. Single mindedness of purpose, incisive thought but too intense and liable to breakdown if over-worked or over-stimulated.

Shallow, wide lines show a shallow, easily swayed temperament. On prints there is some difficulty in recognizing whether lines are deep but extended with pressure or naturally wide; only experience can really teach the difference.

When the lines look faded, as though rubbed out, they tell a warning of serious mineral deficiency which will be fully considered in Chapter V, Part IV. Paleness in colour, and if the hand is stretched lines appear to lie in a pale, or white valley, has a kindred message as I have proved on my own hands.

A hand showing very few lines has not much cortical representation of its nervous system. Extreme examples may be found on the hands of African tribesmen among whom even babies can survive burns that would cause a European to die of shock. The men often have great difficulty in exactly locating an unseen pain and arise after operations in a most surprising manner, if their imagination can be captured.

Obviously, for countless generations they must have bred from stock that could survive the perils of bush life, and have kept a high resistance to pain.

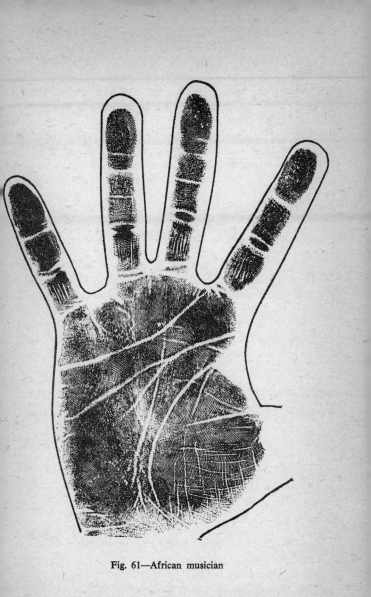

Fig. 61—African musician

An equal paucity of lines may be seen on the hands of men who endure great hardships with no ill effects, but in Britain, at any rate, one cannot just say 'farmers and sailors'. One of the most beautiful pair of hands I have seen was owned by a country blacksmith.

Many lines wandering about a palm at random are called a 'Barbed wire entanglement' by a Fellow of the S.S.P.P., which is an accurate description of the appearance. The condition shows a highly or over-developed nervous system where there is too much response from the nerves. When found on the hands of an outwardly phlegmatic person the multitude of lines portray the unseen and controlled responses—trust the message of the hands and suspect the outward behaviour pattern.

Faults will be studied in detail on the individual lines but the common denominator should be recognized first.

Islands show a divided mind. Think of the electrical impulses crossing the divide in two paths, in 'two minds', the foundation of worry. Whether the two minds are caused by personal anxieties or ill-health must be deduced from the rest of the hand where each line shows its special attitude to the distortion.

Little Cuts across lines suggest inner tensions arresting the flow of autonomic nervous impulses and therefore the normal flow of the juices of the body.

Little Dots on lines are very similar in meaning. There is a suggestion that the cuts suggest annoyance, a check from outside oneself, whereas the dots are from one's own tensions and are affecting health. This is another subject for exact investigation.

Tassels usually appear at the end of lines and, again, must be considered according to their placing, but the general effect is a dissipation of the energy represented by the line.

Fraying also dissipates energy, but when a line is continuous so that the fraying is only formed by little branches the condition only shows a variety of interests.

Where there is no backing of a continuous line the pattern suggests the work of the line is being interrupted, disconnected, so that encouragement must be given to the owner to make the effort to concentrate his energies, plus a careful enquiry as to health.

Breaks also indicate a lack of continuity; the surrounding conditions should be noted carefully, as also the direction and appearance of the line before and after the break.

These general rules about lines can be safely applied wherever lines appear, even in unconventional place and direction. The areas of the hand, mounts, fingers, etc., each have their correlation with a part of the personality. The strength and depth of the lines show the cortical awareness of that facet as operating at that moment in the life of the owner of the hand studied.

CHAPTER II

TRANSVERSE LINES

The Head (Proximal Transverse Line)

When glancing at a palm to assess how best to work with a new colleague, conduct an interview and so on, the Head Line demands first attention as it shows the way an owner thinks—is he original, factual, imaginative, grasping? A great deal may have already been observed according to the principles of Chirognomy, but this line indicates how he will use his potentials.

Noel Jaquin (lecture to the S.S.P.P. 1946) called this line 'the compass of the hand' and in all the years since I have found no reason to dispute his designation. Basically the line may be taken as showing the amount of energy available to the brain together with the scope and direction whence the cortex will seek, use, and store what information it may require. Of course the Head Line must be read in conjunction with other signs because a photographic memory can pass examinations without very much grasp of the subject of which the owner *seems* to have learnt so much. A Member of the S.S.P.P. (India) sent in the prints of several successful candidates for a difficult examination. They all showed the short factual type of Head Line. The master did not say whether the candidates could apply their knowledge.

People of apparently feeble intellect may have a well engraved Head Line yet through a poor heart, inadequate metabolism, or bodily injuries they cannot bring their mental powers into use.

To be strictly accurate the transverse lines have neither

beginning nor end in the palm; the 'ends' are between palm and brain. Lines can change at either side of the hand or anywhere along the course. But the terms 'beginning and end' are so habitual that it is difficult not to use them.

The most permanent part of the Head Line, usually known as the 'Beginning' may be found anywhere between the ring around the thumb and the fore-finger. Half-way between the digits, lightly touching or just not touching the Life Line is

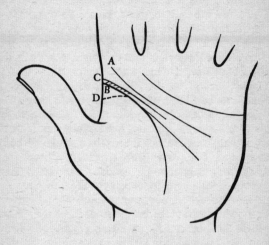

Fig. 62—Head Line, beginning

the position of balance. When found in this location thinking will be clear, free from emotion but not arrogant or self-willed.

When completely free of the Life Line, lying up on the Mount of Jupiter, thinking will be done from one's own judgement. The wide gap between Head and Life shows too much independence of mind, of appreciation of the self, leading to impetuousness and impulsiveness when young. Self-reliance is an asset when the self is wise enough to be relied upon, so the youngster should be encouraged to judge wisely, perhaps teased for any silly mistakes, for there is little hope of making him careful by nature. The advantage of the gap, when suitably tempered by wisdom, is clarity of mind. Because they support their own judgement they do not allow sentiment to creep in and spoil decisions. Not all separated Head Lines are ruthless, with a good Heart Line they may develop understanding, even sympathy, but no one can be ruthless in *cold blood*, without the Head Line veering towards the Mount of Jupiter.

The clinging line (Fig. 62, b), which does not part company with the Life Line until they have passed an imaginary boundary drawn from the division between the Index and Medius fingers, has many adjectives in old-fashioned books on Palmistry, the root of them all is that the thinking finds its source in the area of emotion. Thoughts are only clear and incisive by a great effort of will so that the owners do indiscreet things they know to be foolish through sentiment. They are unable to cause pain because they feel hurt so keenly themselves.

This form is not conducive to absolute truth. The owners do not actually tell lies but the truth, if it should be hurtful, is wrapped in cellophane with a bow of ribbon. This tied Head Line may be seen on the hands of a surprising number of men, many of whom would hate anyone to know how sensitive they are. With such emotions as resentment and hurt feelings, especially when advantage has been taken of their thoughtfulness, their thinking can be mixed up emotionally with anger or fear as it was affected in kindly ways and become the kindle to fire red, hot-blooded nails or to freeze the ice around the pale, square ones. When someone with a tied Head Line has to, for instance, dismiss an employee the announcement will be postponed as long as possible in the hope that some good excuse will turn up. This can give rise to misunderstandings of motives so that the very people are aggrieved to whom the tied Head Line is trying to be kind.

Between these two extremes there are two alternatives (Fig. 62, c). The middle plane which, as we have seen, allows neither self-will nor emotion to interfere with the lucidity and wisdom of decision. Problems are seen in the most balanced way possible within the capacity of the owner.

Sometimes the line itself or a strong branch rises from the

Mount of Mars and crosses the Life Line from the thumb side (Fig. 62, d). This line tells some story of a conscious need of courage. Leaders who are afraid of being afraid or of showing their fear; people engaged in slow timed, calculated hazards; children who are afraid of parents or school may grow a branch as they combat the emotion of which they are ashamed. When seen only on the left hand this branch may represent a very great admiration for the quality of physical courage.

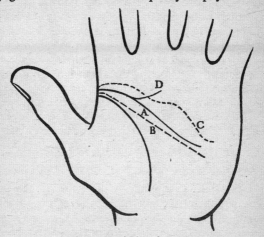

Fig. 63—Head Line, the course

I think this line shows a conscious awareness of need for courage in contrast to the instinctive admiration for the quality shown by the skin pattern on the Mount of Mars. This is a feeling, not even a hypothesis, but the pattern in the skin seems more joyous while the line seems more duty bound.

On the right hand only the appreciation of courage might have been inherited from one parent, but the line could have been acquired by some event such as standing up to a bully at school; the line has registered a protest without having upset the personality.

We think the need for courage to face the world is felt too strongly when a deep line from Mars is the *only* 'beginning' of the Head Line, there is a danger of becoming anti-social.

The Course

Across the hand the line may arch as a bow (a) or be drawn straight as by a ruler (b), or waver uncertainly along its path. These divergencies speak for themselves—a straight line will want to 'see straight'—truth at any price; while the curved one will have more springiness, more capacity for original ideas. The wavering line (Fig. 63, c) shows the thoughts lured by the various fingers to be influenced by the need for appreciation, preoccupation with mundane values, or vanity. This waviness is an important indication that all is not well with the child, he lacks a sense of security to enable him to be himself (or his world is not secure and he cannot find himself at home in it). A stronger minded youngster grows branches up towards the fingers to display his resentment—the very curve of the branch (Fig. 63, d) follows the curve of the hind legs of a kicking donkey! Unjustly treated grown-ups can grow these branches too, which fade when they feel that justice has been restored to them.

The Percussion End

When the Head Line is above the centre of the palm all feeling is cut out of thought. Straight across, the line acts as a barrier dividing brain and warmth. It may actually

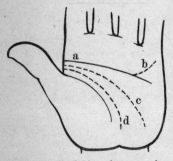

turn up towards the fingers thus taking every bit of feeling out of the picture (Fig. 64, a). Turning up towards the little finger shows the Head Line's concern with financial aspects. Thinking is received and expressed on a material plane, with the result that it is always alert for gain.

A little upwards hook is

Fig. 64—Head Line, the percussion end

sometimes found on a hand which shows no other aptitude for the control of money (Fig. 64, b). This little hook I have named the 'sixpenny hook' because it comes on the hands of women who have to be careful of the sixpences. I have known it to vanish when conditions have improved, and I consider that it shows that the enforced carefulness is really alien to the character.

When the line ends in the farthest corner of the Mount of Luna (Fig. 64, c) thought will be coloured with racial and ancestral memories to allow a rich and fanciful imagination.

When such a long line follows the curve of the Life Line, almost parallel to it, there will be a much warmer love of life and of people; writers will express themselves in more romantic stories, the imagination will be used for more humanitarian interests which can become too emotional (Fig. 64, d). Some books have suggested that these long lines show suicidal tendencies, but none of my half-dozen prints of people who have left, or have attempted to leave, this world by their own hands, show a specially long or emotional Head Line.

Long, clear Head Lines can be used for creative invention as on the Society's casts of George Bernard Shaw and published pictures of the prints of Professor Einstein and Sir Winston Churchill, to mention but three. The imagination must be used and controlled by strong thumbs to fulfil all their promise. Uncontrolled, while not consciously being untruthful, an accident involving two cars and the tempers of three people becomes a group of cars and injured bodies complete with the colours of the cars, clothes, stains on the road! A reply 'Oh, just let me finish this letter' can become a mortal insult with a long conversation of 'he saids'. But how dull the world would be without some over-long and drooping Head Lines.

Here again the line itself may be straight with the droop in general direction only when accuracy will control imagination and a very high degree of observation may be developed (Fig. 65, a).

Short

A Head Line may be short, only clearing the Medius finger; when deep and clear it shows a thought process limited to mundane affairs but excellent for business routine and well suited to a square hand. A short line on a long hand with pointed fingers makes one pause to consider whether the nails and fingers are becoming the talons mentioned under Nails (page 77, Part I, Chapter V).

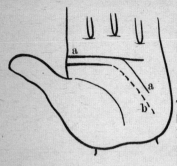

Fig. 65—Head Line, more endings

This business-type line, especially with conic or spatulate finger tips, may make a sudden, sharp droop under the Apollo finger. The owner will be practical in worldly things but intensely interested in the Arts. This formation may show a business man who collects or has some feeling for the Fine Arts, or the antique dealer or diamond merchant himself.

Unused (Fig. 65, b)

When Head Lines are deep for a short way and have a faint unused-looking line going on towards the sub-conscious side of the hand they show the people who have had dreams but have had to concentrate very strongly on earning a living. They always feel frustrated as though they know they are missing something which their sense of duty will not allow them to seek. It is well to encourage such lines to find a hobby where they can use the latent artistry or imagination. Also, if possible, explain to their partners in life how necessary and urgent such a hobby is. So tragically often a gift which would give interest and happiness to the possessor is discouraged by a selfish, thoughtless or jealous family into expressing itself as a duodenal ulcer.

Forked

The line may terminate in a fork, one branch lying more or less straight across the Mount of Mars Negative and the other drooping on to Luna. This is known as the 'Writer's

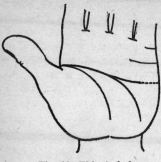

Fig. 66—Writer's fork

Fork' but the basic meaning is that the imagination can be used for practical ends. The formation may express itself equally well as a commercial artist, a skilled window dresser, a dress designer, or a maker of artistic pottery. Should either fork attain the edge of the skin pattern on the outside of the hand Indian tradition claims that the work of the head shall be known across the sea; I have found this to be true on many occasions when the work has been outstanding.

Should the branches of the fork be excessively wide apart, say about sixty to ninety degrees, the two ways of thinking are excessively wide apart as well and will find difficulty in working smoothly together. There may be a tendency to alternate the interests instead of imagination finding expression in practice. Both sides would be happier if they could find a common meeting ground.

Texture

An ultra fine Head Line is a warning that it must not be worked too hard *continuously* but when tired a short rest of the cup-of-tea-and-cigarette order will enable it to recuperate. If this fine line is forced it will cease to exchange clear messages with the brain and the work will be incorrect or muddled and delayed. When overcharged with emotion this type of line is liable to fuse in the same way as an electric iron wired for 100 volts behaves when put on a 225 volt circuit. I think the fine line explains how brains wired to exact, precise, business-type thinking erupt in race riots and destruction when overexcited by passions. They just cannot *think* at all. (e.g. Fig. 46, page 90).

Wide and shallow lines lead to demonstrations too but through a different cause. Here the thinking is vague, imprecise and easily swayed. The simile is that of a wide, shallow river whose waters respond to the passing breeze but can become smooth again equally quickly. So in personal life, these wide shallow lines can be very charming to meet, good at instinctive thoughts but a little apt to forget all about any subject or plan when the discussion is over (example, Fig. 61, page 137).

Islands within the Head Line carry their usual meaning

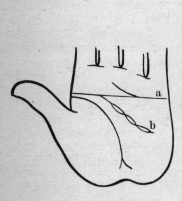

Fig. 67—Simian Line and islands on   Fig. 68—Living example
          Head Line branch

of worry (Fig. 67, b), but may, if a series and forming a chain, indicate a deficiency of the essential mineral salt potassium of which the brain and nerves need a good supply. This type of islanding is often accompanied by a tiresome loss of memory which is purely physical and can be restored by a suitable tonic. There is some reason for suspecting that one island under the finger of Saturn relates to business worry, especially when it occurs at the junction with the Fate Line, but I have not found the reading one hundred per cent reliable. There is also a tradition that a star on the Head Line where it is crossed by one of the vertical lines means a head injury. So far I have not found this reading entirely correct either but on heavily lined hands a cross is difficult to differentiate from the chance crossings of lines which keep their individual meanings.

Little dark dots on the line are all too frequent signs of worry, the nagging anxiety which stops one thinking properly. With a right-handed person they follow the rule by appearing first on the right-hand, then both, and clearing in the same order so that when seen on the left hand only, one can congratulate the owner on having resolved the anxieties within the last six to ten months; or, if on the right hand, try to help them before the left becomes involved.

The Head Line (Fig. 67, 68) can unite into one line with the Heart Line above, forming but one channel across the hand for a great part of the way. This formation is often known as the Simian Line and is a sign of concentrative power. The owners expend all their energy on one thing at a time. If engrossed in a task they will appear to forget all else until the task is completed. They love with the same intensity, so the wife of a man with Head and Heart Lines conjoined on both hands must identify herself with her husband's career in order to find any happiness. This single line is shown at its best when, in spite of forming one line across the palm, a branch rises to form the conscious end of a Heart Line and another branch drops from the single bar to form the more aesthetic part of the Head Line (Fig. 67, b). This can give far-sightedness or imagination according to whether the paths of the branches be direct or arched.

Colour in the Head Line is important but is fully dealt with in Chapter VII on Health.

Heart (Upper Transverse) Line   *(Distal Transverse Crease)*

The Heart Line is responsible for carrying the forces of the palm to give life to the instinctive thinking of the fingers.

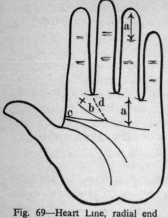

Fig. 69—Heart Line, radial end

It should measure the same distance from the boundary of fingers two, three and four as the length of the top phalange of each respective finger (Fig. 69, a). Sometimes the line is a little nearer to the fingers when the nail section of the fourth digit is exceptionally long but the nail phalange length is a good standard for normality. The fruit of the tree of the palm and the fruit of the tree of the fingers are then in harmony. Take an imaginary line from the centre of the third finger to the Heart Line beneath; from there to the percussion is solely concerned with the physical pump and with the quality of the blood that is passing through that organ.

From the same point towards the first finger side of the palm it represents the conscious emotional aspect of the heart. The division is not exact, the two pictures merge a little as they clear the Apollo finger. A line may show strains and stresses towards the outside of the palm but become a clean, clear line of directed affection as it appears under the finger of Saturn. A good, long heart line is essential for anyone to feel *love* or enthusiasm but that emotion may be directed in several ways.

Where two or more hand-interpreters are gathered together there will be argument about the beginning and ending of the Heart Line. As with the Lower Transverse Line the real connection is between hand and brain, but in this case of the Upper Line the part under the little finger tends to remain static in position, only changing in texture, while the Radial end may show considerable changes in accordance with emotional crises and attitudes. The line may be found in several different positions under or towards the Index finger.

1. (Fig. 69, b). Lying straight on to the Mount of Jupiter, especially if touching or towards the apex of the skin pattern, the emotional force is carried to the concept of Self.

When this line is unaccompanied by any branches the owners love themselves and insist on the object of their affections being worthy of them. Politely, this position is called 'Idealism'. A branch in this direction is very helpful as it ensures fastidiousness in the moral outlook: but if there be but one single line which takes this course there is a tendency to be more generous-minded than loving.

2. (Fig. 69, c). Should the line continue across the Mount of Jupiter, passing well below the apex, sometimes even to the boundary of the skin pattern, the emotional force is carried to the outside world. This formation is frequently found on the hands of District Officers of the Colonial Service and such-like devoted men to whom the people in their care are their all. This type of line, or a branch from the Heart Line in this direction, should be on the hands of anyone who is personally responsible for other people as a group.

One, single linear extension to the Heart Line across to terminate between thumb and Index is another warning to wives that they will always be of secondary importance to work; but if the wives have the mark too and hold some position such as Red Cross Commandant or similar responsibility, there will be complete understanding between the couple. A bearer of this form told me that he thought he felt more *devotion* to his wife than demonstrable affection.

3. (Fig. 69, d). Curving up to between first and second fingers, even to the edge of the skin pattern.

The warmth of affection indicated by the generous curve is almost self-explanatory—affection is shared between Self and the World. At its best the line will stop just short of the edge of the skin pattern by perhaps one quarter of an inch when the owner will be able to know the heights and depths of emotion. The world may be well lost for love.

When found on the hands of children the rich curve demonstrates their need of some display, of some assurance of affection. I have seen this curving line many times on the hands of young people who have been in trouble at school by being uninterested and generally unco-operative. When we have discussed their need for love they have proved to have thought that, for various reasons, their parents did not love them, in sum a real 'woolly worms in the garden' attitude. Their whole world changed when they understood why they had to go to school while parents went abroad, when they understood why Mother could not show her sadness in case 'Small' broke down·too. (Parents have to be persuaded to relax the extreme stiffness of the upper lip also!) My first happy example who

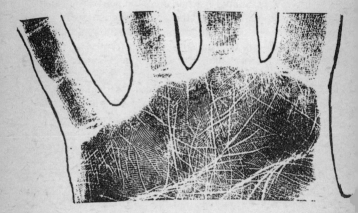

Fig. 70—A good example

taught me this lesson might have been a completely different person, his whole heart became set on helping Mummy to be brave.

When the line between the fingers extends to the edge of the skin pattern I have found it to indicate possessiveness: including the stultifying jealousy of a mother who cannot let her children grow up, finds fault with every young friend they bring home who might be a possible candidate for matrimony. The tragedy lies in the owner of this over-long, possessive Heart Line honestly thinking the reactions arise from the most high-minded and conscientious motives. The tendency is increased by an imaginative Head Line but can be ameliorated by a sense of humour which recognizes the symptoms. Should this excessive Heart Line have even a small branch towards the Mount of Jupiter the owner will sincerely think that no one is quite good enough for his or her offspring.

Such are the dangers, the compensation lies in knowing heights of love which can be sublimated into intense enthusiasm for an objective. Should the Fate Line, or a branch therefrom join this high Heart Line there is a propitious indication for an ambitious and successful career.

The ideal Heart Line (Fig. 70), has a three-pronged fork beginning as the line crosses the padding between the first two fingers.

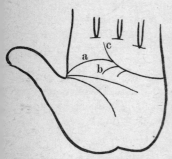

Fig. 71—Heart Line, further radial ends

4. (Fig. 71, a). Dropping on to the Head or Life Lines. Should the Heart Line attain the Mount of Jupiter and thence drop to the Life and Head Lines, looking as though it had been hit down by something from outside, there is mirrored some feeling of disappointment or disillusionment which experience has led to a greater understanding of the unhappiness of other people. The lesson of understanding and sympathy has been accepted.

5. (Fig. 71, b). Natural kindness is assured when a branch from the Heart Line either joins or points towards the Head Line. Such a branch seems to convey the warmth of the heart to the thinking. Should the branch leave the main line under the Apollo finger the kindness must be appreciated and applauded. When the branch leaves under the finger of Saturn I have known the kind thoughts to appear grudgingly given, almost secretive. For acceptance a quick, almost equally secret, recognition is in order as long as there is no possibility of embarrassment.

6. A Heart Line can be so short as to stop abruptly under the Medius finger. These people like rather than love, they can be good and loyal friends but do not feel the same personal emotion; they demand companionship as the primary importance from their partners. The over-short line is not very helpful for enthusiasms and can sometimes give up, especially under health strains. Again be careful in the interpretation and make sure that there is not a faded or neglected line continuing from it as someone who has had misfortunes, and feels they can never love anyone else, may carry this marking.

7. (Fig. 71, c). Should the line turn sharply upwards under Saturn finger and end either between the fingers but strongly towards the side of the second finger, or directly under that finger, all the Jupiterian influence of self-pride and fastidiousness is lacking, people are loved whether they are worthy or not. This formation is very susceptible to the lure of mates from a different social background and promotes physical allure to the first consideration. They make sympathetic parents and find it easy to be forgiving and helpful no matter what scrapes may be confessed.

Mrs. St. Hill postulated that a line which lay deep into the palm under the third finger showed the quality of Mercy. We of the S.S.P.P. fully endorse this reading and suggest further that a Heart Line obviously high on the palm suggests emotion of brain rather than of heart.

The vagaries of the physical aspect of the Heart Line will be discussed in Chapters IV and V, Part IV, pages 240-249 but some signs should be mentioned in connection with ordinary interpretation.

This Upper Transverse Line is responsive to the dangers of worry which is signified by dots and cuts. On this line these signs indicate worries about or for other folk. I do not like to see them on a hand because the heart being such an important pumping organ, it is essential for health that the fluids should be free to flow in their correct piping. The dots and cuts show tensions which are impeding the flow.

Islands

An island under the third finger is associated with eye trouble but I think it will be proved to refer to those eye troubles caused by mineral imbalances. Towards the fourth finger under the inner side of that digit, any danger indicated will be to the teeth. Some practitioners think hearing imperfections may be shown by an island in the Heart Line under Saturn, but I await conviction as I cannot dissociate the Medius line from the skeletal and digestive systems. Possibly any osseous trouble affecting hearing is shown thus—one of many subjects yet to be proved.

Girdle of Venus

Before leaving the transverse lines of the palm it would be well to consider that line which sometimes lies across the upper part of the palm between fingers and Heart Line and

is known as the 'Girdle of Venus'. It is as if the main cable of the Heart Line were not properly insulated and excited a secondary cable in the mind.

There may be one single line or a series of broken ones, The more usual position is encircling the mounts of Saturn and Apollo but there may be an extension to include the Mount of Mercury as well. The

Fig. 72—Girdle of Venus

Girdle does not include the area of Jupiter. Conic and pointed fingers with a narrower type of hand are the natural habitat, so that should the Girdle be found on a square or spatulate fingered hand the influence will prove dominant in the character.

The Girdle is a *gift* with all the responsibilities attached to any gift, including that of proper use. The line enables life to be injected into any object of the mind. This is not quite the same thing as imagination for the effect of the Girdle can be seen with a most practical, direct type of Head Line; but when a person, an animal or a thing is considered it becomes alive, a personality. A pet, a machine, is seen with a character of its own—and not infrequently a name. For example this line is invaluable to a writer whose characters will live in the memory as live people; bird-watching becomes the intimate doings of a special bird family nesting in the apple tree which, in turn, is a familiar friend.

Misused, the gift increases the danger of adventures beyond the moral code—a badly brought up poodle can be so very much more naughty and tiresome than many other breeds simply because it can see so many more ways of being tiresome. So, in young people, once they decide to be 'bad' they can see such wonderful ways of carrying out their intentions.

On the negative side, left unused, the gift can degenerate into an 'If only' attitude. We all have to choose between paths from time to time and no path is without some difficulties. This line or lines can make the rejected path appear so wonderful that we do not make the best of the path we have chosen. Remind the owner of a strong Girdle to envisage all the dire things that could have happened, which he saw when he made his decision and cut that unhappy phrase right out.

One of the most charming Girdles I have seen belonged to a man in a Pensions Office. Tiresome old woman No. 000,000 became in his eyes, poor old Mrs. 'Dash' as he filled in her forms for her and explained what she had to do. He was glad personally when he was able to make her comfortable. All his pensioners lived in his mind as human beings.

One, unbroken line is more self-centred than the more broken-up form, better suited to a dramatist or producer. The kindly benefactor of Mrs. Dash had a number of little lines forming the arc.

Sometimes when the pattern is continued across the base or the Mount of Mercury to the 'marriage' lines it suggests a dramatization of marriage and social contacts.

When the Girdle of Venus accompanies a long, imaginative Head Line every effort should be made to engage in some form of creative work; the actual choice of the use of the gifts will follow the shape of finger tips, palm, skin pattern and so on, but there are few aspects of creative work which cannot benefit by imaginative visualization.

CHAPTER III

VERTICAL LINES

The Life or Thumb Line (Radial Longitudinal)

The Life Line, unlike the horizontal lines, does start and end; there is a capacity for making considerable changes. The line can grow, especially if it lies in the groove of the skin pattern; it can also shorten, become tasselled, suffer any or all of the vagaries to which a line is susceptible.

The conventional way to read Time from this line is to start from the boundary of the palmar pattern beneath the Index finger and read downwards towards the wrist. This is the more satisfactory way because clear, even drastic, changes occur towards the wrist end, while a modest branch is all that may be thrown out at the digital end. The eminent German, Julius Spier measured from the wrist upwards, and of course his pupils follow his interpretation, but I think we shall find the cause of this reading when we study Fate and Mercury Lines.

Many errors are made in timing through insufficient care in using the true commencement, the actual boundary of the palm, but Time will be considered in detail at the end of this Part III.

The Life Line does *not* show the length of life, but it does show our expectation of enjoyment of life, of the awareness of being alive. There are many people with a vague, tasselled ending who remain on this earth through the excellence of their digestive systems. A strong, clear Life Line may break up, island, or fade out after a serious accident; or remain clear and long on the hand when the owner has had a fatal encounter with a motor car. Some exceptions have been noted as when young men, before both World Wars, seemed to be destined to a short life, but these examples are rare.

The Life Line shows *awareness of the life force* as gauged by the Mount of Venus. If this basic meaning is kept in sight the line is not difficult to interpret.

Commencement

Starting from the boundary of the skin pattern the line may lie high up under the Mount of Jupiter (Fig. 73, a) when the owner will show the urge to realize the best that is in him, a

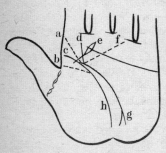

Fig. 73—Life Line, beginning

good ambition. The opposite extreme is from deep down on the Mount of Mars (Fig. 73, b) when there is an unsureness which has to call on conscious courage to face life and combat the instinctive trends towards anti-social withdrawal from life. A branch, if not the actual line itself, may be engraved from the Mount of Mars when an explorer or a soldier is afraid of showing fear, and I once saw such a branch on the hands of a spy.

The comfortable mean would be just about half-way between the crease line at the base of the Index finger and the 'Family Ring' at the movement crease of the thumb (Fig. 73, c).

For the first twenty years, as the line passes under the Mount of Jupiter (concept of self) the story of the life is mainly concerned with growth and education. Efforts and ambitions are shown by lines rising from it, usually to the Mount of Jupiter (Fig. 73, d). Should the rising lines direct themselves to other mounts they may be interpreted accordingly. If branch lines proceed to Saturn there has probably been effort or worry about the domestic background, especially when this effort line takes the form of a very long 'worry' island (Fig. 73, e). Some Chirologists see a line leaving the Life Line under Jupiter and lying towards the Saturn finger as a 'Father's line' and certainly I had my own father described accurately, but he was a Saturnian type so I am not sure of this reading. It may be interesting to inquire how often this suggested 'Father's line' proves correct.

Directed to the Mount of Apollo a branch line suggests some early bid for success, so one seeks corroboration on the Fate or Sun Lines (Fig. 73, f).

The Life Line usually has a slightly herring-bone effect at the beginning for the child is absorbing impressions from all sides, but these lines of special effort are unmistakable. The effort may not be very dramatic in the eyes of the world; but such a rising line shows the effort output of the owner. Thus an over-sensitive or parent-dominated child may put out an effort line when he goes to boarding school or faces the 'eleven-plus' examination, while in another, surer, hand the meaning might be the winning of a scholarship.

Once past childhood the line may take one of three courses. It may sweep boldly out into the palm (Fig. 73, g) it may cling to the Family Line round the joint of the thumb as though afraid to leave the family; or the middle way, quietly encircling the muscles of the thumb (Fig. 73, h).

The sweep of the line is of enormous importance with regard to recuperative powers whether necessitated by circumstance or health. A poor line giving no breadth to the Mount of Venus (Thenar Eminence) shows poor arterial palmar arches and a poor vitality. A Member of the S.S.P.P. was the Casualty Sister in a big provincial hospital. She related how she always looked at the sweep of the Life Line when a patient was safely in bed. If the line lay well out into the hand she was sure of the patient's co-operation, he would try to remain alive; but if the line was close into the thumb she had a 'Special' nurse to watch him through the night and, without fail, the early hours of the morning found him giving up the will to live, even if he had only a broken leg.

This reading is equally true psychologically. The widely spaced Venus will surmount emotional or business setbacks in the same way, postponing any abandonment of his plans till after tomorrow's post.

A poorly placed Life Line can also impoverish the quantity

of emotion available to the Heart Line. People can love deeply with their minds when the Heart Line is generously curved but they can be discontented, disappointed with their partners because they themselves have not the physical warmth to put into the alliance. On the whole a poor sweep to the Life Line suggests a reluctance to marry.

As ever the middle path is balanced, warm but not too adventurous and often ends or has a fork around the base of the thumb.

Course

Having noted the general direction of the line we can study the messages that may be carried along the course.

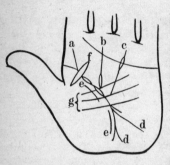

Fig. 74—Life Line, the course

Lines arising from the Life Line are always effort lines (Fig. 74, a, b, c). On most hands subsidiary lines tend to go downwards after the age of about fifty so rising lines in the latter part of the course are of primary importance. Again we can follow the rules of direction. Those towards Jupiter indicate some form of ambitious effort; towards Saturn may be connected with business but usually the thought of some destined duty shadows the effort. Towards Apollo the effort lines become a form of Sun Line which we will be studying in detail in Chapter IV, but think of the meaning as some expression of happiness, possibly fame or fortune.

Fine lines dropping towards the outer side of the palm may mean a wish to travel but they are rather elusive and may disappear in the course of a few weeks. The basic meaning should be read as a discontent with present circumstances, a wish to be free. Only very clear, long branches can be interpreted as a wish actually to travel (Fig. 74, d).

Little breaks in the Life Line are remembrances or warnings of breaks in the tenor of life. Note whether the disruptions are protected by a square or an inside line looking like a splint to the main line (Fig. 74, e). The square and the splint line show a danger of some sort either surmounted or avoidable.

Islands

Sometimes there is quite a sequence of islands within the line itself (Fig. 74). This may denote ill-health or over worry, or both. For instance one recent example arose from persistent overwork on the hands of a woman who just could not stop worrying and getting 'worked-up'.

Another cause of a chained effect can be persistent insomnia but that condition has other signals as well, to be discussed on page 237 and in Fig. 58.

An island crossing the Life Line (Fig. 74, f) is also an indication of worry, usually financial, especially when directed towards the Mount of Saturn. When the family is involved the island can start almost from the Family Ring and stretch right on to the base of the Medius finger, the two sides encompassing the period of acute anxiety.

Should a similar island be directed towards Apollo the meaning would be a memory or fear of disgrace in the eyes of the world. On hands where the danger lies ahead the island may be a warning that trouble could be avoided if the owner would readjust his mental outlook. Whatever you think about the sign, do try to find, from the hand, what weakness could cause such a warning to be necessary and explain that it is the owner's super-conscious-Self trying to get him to avert the disaster in time.

The period of the middle years, of building and endeavour, lies across the area of Mars below the finger of Saturn. Lines rising from the Life Line in this position show the direction and cost of the endeavour, as distinct from the crossing lines from the Mount of Venus which speak of changes *not* of one's own choosing (Fig. 74, g).

With a Life Line which lies far out into the palm the Fate Line sometimes branches from it at about the period representing fifty or sixty years of age. This will be considered with the Fate Line but I have seen this very large 'effort' when, owing to the taking up of some interest or other cause life has, in fact, 'blossomed' at fifty.

Note whether a restricted Fate Line has been clinging to the thumb and is just emerging, or whether it is, in truth, a great new effort line.

Ending

When the Life Line ends around the thumb it shows a love of home, preferably in the native land. When this formation is only on the right hand, with the left line across the palm, the life will be lived in home surroundings but the dreams will be of travel. When the formation is accompanied by a very deep, long career line duty has heavily restricted inward longings.

Reversed, the Life Line around the left thumb with the right hand line engraved across the palm, life will take the owners to distant places but they will have a hidden yearning, perhaps not apparent in daily life, which they will compensate by making a 'home' wherever they find themselves. Should the tie be withdrawn, left hand home-clinging folk will take the first plane back to the land of their birth that funds permit. If frustrated in their longing beware depression, they must have a shell to retreat into.

The Life Line may end towards, or well on to, the Mount of the Moon. This denotes a love of adventure, of meeting new people, going to new places and taking up new ideas. This tendency is shown up vividly when the thumb is flexible at the top joint; any adventure that comes their way will be entered into with zest and, usually, they are equable travellers taking the rough as an adventure, or subject for a good story, yet being grateful and sybaritic for the smoother parts. Stiffer thumbs seem to plan the journeys more deliberately but that may be prejudice, as I have known several archaeologists with adventurous Life Lines and persistent thumbs.

A fork shows a life divided between home and far places. However much they may enjoy travel or work in the sun, the call of home, of the conditions and surroundings of childhood, will always be with them so that they dream of returning home directly the task is ended. When they do retire and settle in their homes they are liable to have tingling toes and want to travel again if only on holiday tours, or, endorsing the duality of the fork, just winter in the sun.

Should the Life Line end in a tassel of fine lines there is a warning of dissipation of nervous energy, a loss of power, an old age that may continue existence on a good digestion. An old friend expressed it as 'Why doesn't God want me since I can't get up and be useful?'

Inside the Life Line

So far we have considered lines leaving the Life Line towards the centre of the palm. On the thumb side of the line there

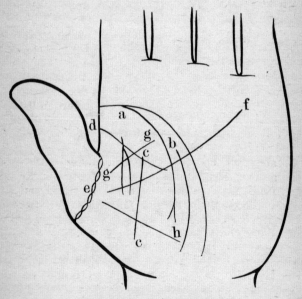

Fig. 75—Inside the Life Line

may be a fork from the Life Line or from a hair line connecting it to the Life Line though actually independent. There may be a line lying very close to the main Life, or several parallel at intervals. Mrs. Robinson made a detailed study of this area in her book *The Graven Palm* to which I would refer readers who are interested.

A line (Fig. 75, a) starting from the Life Line represents either a husband or wife, or someone very closely connected to the home. I have not found it an infallible sign of matrimony, with or without licence, and Mrs. St. Hill recounts how she found an example which could only be representing a beloved dog. However, we can be certain that this line of connected origin indicates a very close influence in the home.

The line (Fig. 75, b) lying close to the Life without actually joining is most easily recognized as a 'Guardian Angel' line. There is a strong feeling of protection which does get the owner through accident and illness as by a miracle. Before the 1939-45 war I saw this mark on the hands of several of the R.A.F. pilots who came through safely; and it was on both the hands of a man who turned his car over three times before it came to rest and he stepped out unhurt. I do not recommend taking undue risks on the strength of such a line, as the distance from the Life Line might have been misinterpreted and the 'Guardian' represent a beloved relative in the home.

Lines farther on to the Venus mount often represent sons and daughters (Fig. 75, c). We can show our anxieties for their success or health which identifies the line with the person.

A rather deep line (Fig. 75, d) rising in the Mount of Mars and crossing toward the Life Line represents someone in the close family—father, mother, sister or brother, who has a great influence on the life. Often fainter lines grow from it, as it were jotting down what happened in the relationship with that member of the family.

Family Ring

Farthest from the Life Line around the base of the thumb is known as the Family Ring (Fig. 75, e); a very well marked one shows a deep interest in the family while it can almost fade out on hands with no family ties. The texture of the ring is usually a chained formation.

Cross Lines on Mount of Venus

From this ring lines of greater or less intensity (Fig. 75, f, g)

cross the Life or are held back by one of the Influence Lines,
or maybe, stop just short of the Life Line itself. Many little
crossings show many changes *not* at the initiative of the
owner. The changes may come from changes of location of
work, from demands by the family; by just being too willing
to accommodate the wishes of others. Opportunities of happiness are vastly improved when such lines are not allowed to

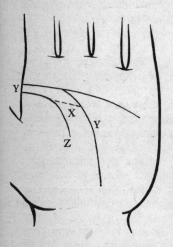

Fig. 76—A modern development

Fig. 77—Living example. See also
pages 170 and 176, Mercury Line

over-encroach. See them as changes and study the texture of
the Life Line before and after the period of crossing.

One simple, strong line (Fig. 75, h) across the Venus mount
but not actually crossing the main line was said by Indian
tradition to threaten the life, as by an enemy. Having seen
it in many African hands subject to strong tribal loyalties, and
also met the line on other hands exceedingly unlikely to be
knifed by an enemy, I have come to credit the line with the
meaning of strong loyalty to whatever takes the place of 'tribe'
to the owner—church, regiment, cricket club, or W.I. can all
show specimens among their loyal and devoted adherents.

There is one aspect, not mentioned in the older books, to

which I would draw attention. During and since the war young people who would have lived more or less sheltered lives have had to change their whole way of life, adjust themselves to a new life pattern using their own brains, character and determination. The Life Line, keeping fairly near the thumb, fades out at about one-third of its expected length (Fig. 76, z) sometimes with a faint hair line across (76, x), sometimes just stopping on a line across from the thumb; sometimes just a fade out. Look further into the palm and it will be seen how sometime during the past ten years often, but not necessarily from the Head Line, another line has started (y) looking, at first glance, like a slightly displaced Fate Line. This indicates that the owner has, from his own initiative, had to choose a fuller life. I have verified this reading on many hands since I first noticed it during the war on the hands of young girls in the Services. In every case there had been some history of a complete change leading to a wider outlook and career.

Fate, Career or Duty Line (Fig. 78, a and b)

The Fate or Career Line in the conventional route goes from the skin pattern boundary at the wrist (Fig. 78, a) on the Mount of Neptune and travels to or through the tri-radii on the Mount of Saturn. Should the line be in this position the career will be found to travel within narrow, dedicated limits. (There is a story that Hitler had this type of Fate Line ending in a sudden death cross at the digital end.)

This type of line is only on the hands of people who follow a prescribed path such as a Civil Servant, devoted nurse or other such dedicated lives. These people believe in Destiny, especially their own, and feel the hand of Fate gripping them and keeping them in a deep, unrelenting groove.

Research by the S.S.P.P. proved that the line in itself is *not* a sign of success or of failure; it is the sign of a life set in a path, which is felt cannot be changed.

Since the line is situated up the middle of the hand, directly under the Medius finger where the preoccupation is with the background to life, the line itself reports on background affairs, the mundane part of the career; the sort of job that is being done or is in mind. Obviously therefore it may be broken, duplicate itself, islands occur, and positive squares may re-assure in troubled periods. Time is measured on the line (page 184, Chapter V) but with limited accuracy.

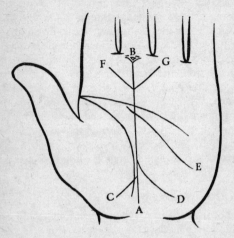

Fig. 78—Fate or Duty Line

Origin

At the wrist end the career may start from any of three sources:

1. The centre of the wrist boundary on the Mount of Neptune. This will impart a self-sufficiency, a balance to the life, and is frequently a deep strong line for as long as it lasts (Fig. 78, a). The value is greatly enhanced when the tri-radii apex of the Neptune mount is dead centre and therefore under the beginning of the line. People who have a line from apex to apex are fatalists in their hearts, even if they deny the charge at first.

2. The Duty line (Fig. 78, c) may start inside the Life Line below the Mount of Venus. Here we see the dominance of the home, a sense of responsibility, of restriction by the family.

When this is the only commencement there is every likelihood of the owner following a parental profession or business and feeling that it is just and right to do so.

Should this restricted beginning join with the line from the centre, the combination will indicate the longing to stand on the owner's own feet, and the pull of the family may be resented. This duality is capable of solution, but if the second foot of the career line begins on the Mount of Luna it is not easily reconciled with the Venusian branch. The two lines may become deep with conflict and one of them may break off early.

3. Any line entering the Fate Line (Fig. 78, d) from Luna represents a completely outside influence coming into the life. At a suitable age, and confirmed elsewhere, the new branch may be a husband or wife, but without confirmation this is not certain. An offer to work at a different pursuit or in another Continent could be marked in the same way. People with such a line are usually connected with a public career.

On the left hand only of a right-handed person this influence line shows a dream, a longing that has not been strong enough to put into practice and can be sublimated as in a library of travel books. On the right hand only the line can speak of a career that is vastly different, while the home life remains in the same milieu—as an example, someone sitting in an office in London working at an export trade with Hong Kong.

When the branch from Luna enters a stabilized career line from Neptune, in both hands, the newcomer may represent some partner or influence coming into the working side of life, and, if the lines continue together as one line, the 'influence' will affect the career. George Bernard Shaw is an example when his marriage gave him the opportunity to turn from journalism to writing the plays which were to make him famous.

If the Influence Line crosses the Fate Line there will be no lasting effect upon the career (Fig. 78, e).

How the line fares after being joined by an Influence branch is most important. Islands show the owner mistrusts the situation and has no hope of success in his heart. Should the line veer towards, or send a branch towards, Apollo there is indeed hope of happiness, and, since happiness lies so very much in oneself, the attainment should be within grasp.

A definite branch in the direction of the little finger suggests there is some business or scientific interest afoot.

Ending

The ideal termination for this Duty Line at the distal end is a trident. The three branches infer the balance of duty, personal satisfaction, and pleasure in the accomplishment. The three branches are rare but two of them making a forked ending are by no means unusual and convey their respective meanings.

The whole line may turn towards the Index finger even, as we saw when studying the Heart Line, merging with an upper branch of the transverse line and enabling the heart to be put into the bid for personal satisfaction and ambition.

The whole line may turn towards Apollo and be found on the hands of a follower of the Arts.

The Mount of Mercury is too far away to lure the whole but branches may cross there when duty is connected with business or science.

Note at what period such divisions and branches break away, remembering that the prospect is vastly improved if the line attains the apex of the relevant mount.

The Fate Line is strongly individualistic, picturing the vagaries of the owner's career. It may stop at one of the transverse lines or even just cease in the Plain of Mars.

Traditionally while the transverse lines retain their meanings a career which stops at either of them is considered to have been dramatically stopped, by errors of head or heart. Sometimes this reading operates but, when stopped at the Heart Line, the age suggests retirement from a life-long occupation and that the owner is seeking what can be made of the remaining years.

Equally a pause at the Head Line may have suggested some freedom from the dull routine and a flight of successful achievement because of the work of the brain.

Great care must be taken to ensure that such a line is really arrested and is not taking over from the Life Line as we noted t the end of the section on the Life Line.

To detail all possible vagaries of the path would be tedious
nd always incomplete but if the reader remembers that a
ne is but an 'awareness' of the habitual path of thought, and
akes care to evaluate all the factors, the milestones of life the
wner wishes to remember or sees ahead will be exactly
nterpreted.

Life Saving Cross

A St. Andrew's Cross sometimes may be seen between the
wo vertical lines about an inch above the wrist. Tradition
ssociates the cross with some achievement in saving life. On
he left hand the effort would be before the mid-thirties, on
he right hand the cross suggests the later part of life, while
n both hands they promise a habit of saving life.

Working at a country fête with the hands of clients thrust
hrough a curtain, every other pair showed the dual crosses.
ater inquiry revealed that they belonged to Nurses from an
vacuated branch of a famous hospital.

Both crosses were very clear on the hands of an Officer in
he Merchant Navy. He had served in Air-Sea Rescue and was
nuch decorated for not only diving in to rescue semi-conscious
irmen but brought them back to life as the launch sped to
ort. Fig. 93, page 217 shows an example. The owner is taking
p a form of 'Fringe Medicine' so the cross may well be
ulfilled.

CHAPTER IV

SUN, MERCURY AND VARIOUS LINES

The Sun Line

The Sun Line may start anywhere on the palm but its destination is the tri-radii apex of the Mount of Apollo.

When Time is estimated upon its length the measurement is really taken from the Duty Line, as the Sun Line either lies directly parallel to or at a close enough angle to retain the age level of the central line.

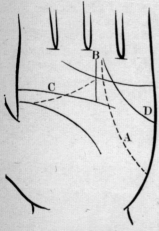

Fig. 79—Sun Line

Success can start from very near to the wrist, from the Duty Line, or clear of it, but such a proximal beginning suggests an infant prodigy. It may spring from the Life, and in fact from anywhere on the palm when the start will pin-point the commencement of some satisfactory happiness.

When this line starts from the Mount of Luna (Fig. 79, a), the source of the satisfaction will be unexpected and the career among people. A career in the public eye.

A perfectly normal Sun Line (Fig. 79, b) can begin at about the level of the Head Line and sometimes may be joined by a line from an earlier part of the Life (Fig. 79, c). When I see this I always ask my subject to think of a thwarted, youthful ambition and seriously to plan how it can be taken up to fill any looming period of retirement. Much satisfaction has been found by attending painting, or musical appreciation classes, or even the more serious study of hands.

When the line is only found above the Heart Line any success will be achieved by the owner's own work. We saw in

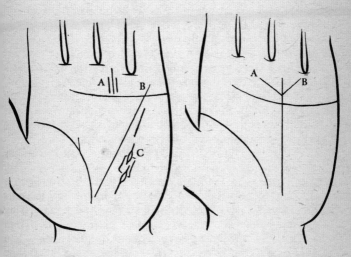

Fig. 80—a: Three lines;   Fig. 81—Ideal Sun Line
   b: Mercury Line;
   c: Broken Mercury Line

the 'Giraffe woman' rings around the finger of Apollo how necessary is a line across the furrows to supply conscious happiness where the spontaneous aspect is cut off.

Three lines above the Heart Line (Fig. 80, a) have a delightful tradition of meaning to which I can subscribe—that the owner will never be 'broke'. Money will always turn up even at the fifty-ninth minute.

More than three lines suggest that too many interests are being followed for the completion of any, and too great a dissipation of energy.

The line taking the Saturn side of the apex unites the idea of happiness with duty; a rather more serious form of interest or study. Should a line tend towards the Mercury side of the apex, or equally a branch in that direction, it has the usual meaning that the field of success in scientific or business achievement is inferred (Fig. 81, b).

Traditionally the ideal Sun Line ends in a neat trident. The line seems to change fairly easily in any part of its length.

A warning—there is a paradox about the Sun Line. Many men and women, eminently successful in the eyes of the world, have no line whatsoever to the Mount of Apollo. These are the perfectionists never satisfied with their own work; never achieving their own dreams. Sometimes the line may show in a modified form on the right hand, an acknowledgement of the plaudits of the world, but the left remains unconvinced and basically modest. I do not know how this works out in a totally left-handed person. On the other hand the Chief of the local Volunteer Fire Brigade may show magnificent specimens.

A line of success and recognition (Fig. 79, d) beginning higher on the palm on the area of Upper Luna and sweeping in a curve on to the Mount of Apollo is a sign of money through inheritance. Fame which, if islanded, might be scandal is accredited to the same position of line when it begins above the Head Line. Clean and clear, it seems to report success but not of one's own making. Again remember the lines may not be factual but show a fear or memory. The basic difference between Fate and Sun Lines lies in the finger mount to which they are directed. When they cross over and change direction the owner is changing his views and attitude to life correspondingly, so do not waste time on names, just follow the meaning when interpreting the message.

Mercury Line

This is a line to which I have given much thought, and feel

that I have thrown some new light upon its interpretation. I regard it as *The Head Line of the Sub-Conscious.*

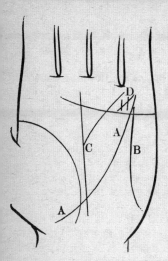

It shows the brain's awareness of the whole sub-conscious system, nervous, autonomic, sympathetic and intuitive response.

When lines in this part of the palm are separated into Hepatica, Business and Intuition there is often great difficulty in deciding which is which. Remembering that any engraving on the percussion must be some awareness of knowledge that is in the mind from the instinctive nervous system, there seems little point in an argument about names. Obviously a line towards the centre of the palm will relate to more mundane affairs while one rising on the Hypothenar Eminence will relate to outside impressions fortified by racial, ancestral and childhood memories.

Fig. 82—Mercury Line

There may be several broken lines, or one strong groove right up to the apex of the Mount of Mercury. When this line continues above the Heart Line the owner will be acutely conscious of his autonomic nervous system, when happy he will feel well, when unhappy there will be a strong sense of malaise. People with this strong awareness of their vagus nerve can overcome difficulties, once they decide to do so, in a most astonishing way.

The line can begin almost anywhere towards the base of the palm and its interpretation is greatly influenced by the position of origin.

Starting from under the thumb on the Mount of Venus, crossing the Life Line and setting out towards the little finger

shows some responsibility for the family in youth (Fig. 82, a).
I have seen it record a childhood dominated by the illness of
a father, a teenage spent nursing a sister, or difficulties in the
home occasioned by an elusive mother. This observation may
be the cause of Julius Spier reading 'Time' on the Life Line
from the wrist upwards but one does wish that he had been
spared long enough to write his projected books on adult
hands.

At the other extreme the line begins low down on the Mount
of Luna when it is known as the 'Line of Intuition' (Fig. 82, b).
This version may end on the Mount of Mars Negative, below
the Heart Line which shows that the intuition is purely instinctive and not really accepted by the brain. Such people are
intensely aware of 'atmosphere' of Earth's radiations, some
examples can psychometrize, but they all use the expression
'I feel'. Should the line pass through the Heart Line to the
mount above it clarifies the knowledge of the message of the
sub-conscious self.

This Mercury Line may route itself more from the centre
of the palm after branching from the Fate or Life Lines.
Living example (Fig. 77, p. 166). Sometimes known as the 'Business Line' it registers worldly acumen, some effort towards
worldly success. This formation may be recognized on the
hands of stockbrokers with a flair for the markets, or manufact-
urers skilled in anticipating fluctuations of fashion or demand.
Among groups of 'hard-headed business men' I have been
astonished by the short, rather poor, but of course single-
minded Head Lines, concentrated on mundane values, not very
good lines in themselves but accompanied by the strong
dominant Line of Mercury showing an instinctive feeling for
the flow of money. Between the two, sometimes starting from
a Life Line that has flung itself across the centre of the palm;
sometimes starting quite clear of other lines, sometimes as high
as just below the Head Line is the so-called 'Liver Line' or
Hepatica. It has but little connection with the liver, but it does
register our awareness of the vagus nerve together with the
autonomic nervous system.

The Mercury Line can lie clear and unsullied to the apex
of the mount, it can be broken, islanded, fading and returning;

it does not show actual illness but our recognition and feelings about our bodies. One classic example, a woman was in hospital after a serious internal operation. She demanded to be shown the line on her hands but the Mercury Line showed no blemish. During the conversation she remarked—'Except for half an hour of dressings time I am enjoying myself here, it is the first real holiday I have had for sixteen years'!' No wonder her sub-conscious self registered no protest.

Operations taken to heart (Fig. 80, c) may show as breaks in the line while islands, as usual, show the worries and anxieties of illness. I have not found an island here, a break or overlap there, to be reliable records of illness at such an age or of a definite organ, but when such mishaps are enclosed within a square the owner feels there has been some form of protection.

Entire absence of this line may be taken as complete indifference to the nervous system, the owner does not know he has one, so the absence of the line is a sign of robust health. There is also little danger from shock as would be felt by the more highly strung folk.

In one of his books Cheiro reads the Mercury Line *towards* the wrist stating that when it crosses the Life Line there is a threat to health. I have seen this crossing on the hands of people who have survived long past the danger point, also of crossings coinciding with illness or accident, so I do not regard the pattern as a reliable source of prognostication but rather as a warning not to try to tell time from the Mercury Line. With all respect to the great Master, Cheiro, I feel sure the modern reading of a responsible childhood is the safe one.

Healing Stigmata

Between the Heart Line and the inside of the little finger there are sometimes three very clearly marked short lines (Fig. 82, d); they can have a cross line uniting them, or one of the lines may be an extension of the Mercury Line, or a branch from the Sun Line. This is the sign of an interest and gift in the art of healing. The sign does not necessarily mean a medical degree, because it denotes a feeling for and an urge to heal, so may occur on the hands of a veterinary surgeon as well as 'fringe' practitioners; when one of the lines is an extension of the Line of Intuition the gift for diagnosis is present. A medical man without these three lines will gravitate to research or some other form of scientific interest. When found on only one hand the three lines may be inherited showing a latent gift from some doctor grandfather or nurse grandmother. When found on both hands of young people who express a wish to study for any of the healing professions they should be encouraged to do so if at all possible.

OTHER LINES

Via Lascivia

A line which may be seen on the lower part of the Mount of Luna lying across to Venus, or coming from the percussion

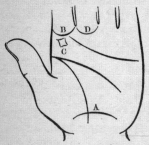

and breaking off before actually crossing the palm, used to be known as the Via Lascivia and credited with dramatic meanings such as a love of drugs or drink, craving for excitement and so on (Fig. 83a, and 104, page 246). These interpretations need mellowing. The line shows such a strong awareness of affinity with Nature that drugs have an undue effect. Allergies

Fig. 83—Other lines. See also Fig. 104, page 246

to penicillin, the mycins and anaesthetics are indicated which are dealt with more fully in Chapter V, Part IV.

The peculiar reaction to alcohol or drugs may explain the bad name this line has earned—if the subject should take too much drink it will exert an extreme influence—but the line usually indicates exactly the opposite, a distaste for such things, the abhorrence of drugs, except for a very occasional aspirin when *in extremis*, is frequently expressed. I have not found any other basic meaning but one of our Members has related some examples with a grandparent who drank.

Homoeopaths frequently show transverse lining on the Mount of Luna. (Chapter V, Part IV.)

Ring of Solomon

A ring of line or lines beneath the Index finger is, traditionally, a sign of wisdom (Fig. 83, b). The ring may form one side of a square on the Mount of Jupiter when value is added to the 'Teacher's Square' where it adds wisdom to knowledge.

Should the Ring form part of a triangle the wisdom is used· in diplomacy.

The Teacher's Square

A neat square under the first finger on the Mount of Jupiter is known by this name (Fig. 82, c). Since squares always bespeak the feeling of security, when one is present at the root of the finger representing our relationship with other people the meaning must be that we feel so secure in our knowledge that we can explain to the not-so-intelligent. While most teachers show this mark there are other uses such as foremen, technicians, Ideal Home demonstrators, and others who have to know their subject well enough to explain simply.

A *Grille* is not a good sign on the mount as it goes with the hypersensitivity of the 'barbed wire entanglement' hand. Quieten the nerves and the square, star or cross will emerge to express themselves.

A *Cross* on the mount (Fig. 85, f) is said to represent a happy and successful marriage in the words of the old song—

> And now she is the lawyer's wife
> And dearly does he love her.
> She lives a happy, successful life
> Far in a station above her.

A *Star* traditionally predicts some sudden and unexpected success when appearing under the first finger. I cannot vouch for the truth of this promise, but the mark is an encouragement!

A strong, clear line up the first finger (as distinguished from the several lines caused by work, dry skin, or age) indicates a very strong feeling of responsibility to other people, hyperconscientiousness. This sense will operate in accordance with which phalanges are most deeply marked. A line from the base will suggest nursing, education, caring for other people, whereas the middle and nail sections strongly marked demonstrates the same feeling about intellectual responsibility.

Ring of Saturn

A ring round the second finger is considerably more rare than the Ring of Solomon (Fig. 83, d). It seems to cut off the useful Saturnian attribute of balance from the whole personality and allows the morose side of the finger full play. This ring can appear after some emotional upheaval and incorporate itself in other lines as the subject becomes readjusted. When an integral part of the pattern of lines on the palm, the owner finds fulfilment in tasks he can pursue away from other people.

Cross

A clear, distinct cross at the side of the nail phalange often signifies a love of and skill with horses. At one dog show I had the opportunity to see the second fingers of many of the breeders and exhibitors who had two or three small crosses instead of one large cross for the larger animals. This is not a serious contribution to the art of Chirology but an observation which might be amusing to follow up.

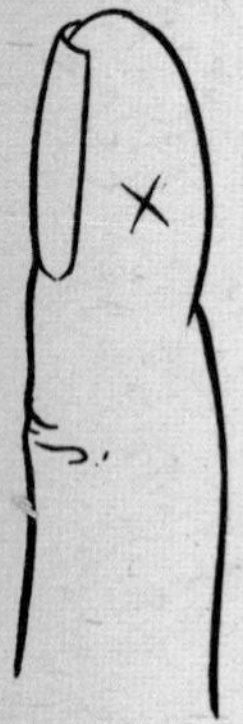

A clear, distinct cross at the end of the Fate Line is, by tradition, a sudden end to the life. The cross must be of the St. Andrew shape and quite distinct from the line itself; and not to be confused with a tree-like branching on the mount which is a very good sign indeed in Hindu lore.

Fig. 84—Skill with animals

A deep clear line up the finger indicates a belief in Destiny; this is especially strong should it form a continuation of the Fate Line itself.

Third Finger

Some students of Chirology might like to discover whether winners of Pools and other large gambles have the traditional star beneath the third finger. Among the half-dozen I have seen only one had a small star practically within the base line of the palmar join, but the other lucky winners had been 'doing the Pools' for a long time with intermittent winnings and regarded the weekly entry as a job. They only showed good, persistent and successful hands.

A *Ring* around the front of the third finger alone is almost unknown. It would merge into the Girdle of Venus (Chapter, II, page 155).

A line up the third finger is equally rare though, logically, should it be present, it would indicate a devotion to some art form.

MARRIAGE AND CHILDREN

No book on Hands would be complete without some allusion to the horizontal lines from the percussion on to the mount below the little finger. They are in the *mental* area of the palm

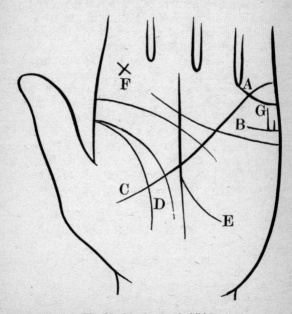

Fig. 85—Marriage and children

so they must show our mental approach to the subject. They do not necessarily show the number of 'affairs'. Since the tradition comes from India where Bride and Groom may not have met before the ceremony, the accent is on the Establishment, the home they are planning to start. When these lines are regarded as *home-making* a high degree of accuracy can result. A furnished flat or service 'quarter' does not show, it must be somewhere with an atmosphere of 'Home' created by oneself.

(a). A line (Fig. 85, a) turning up towards the little finger —like a Ring of Solomon on the opposite side of the hand—is supposed to be the sign of a bachelor or spinster.

(b). A line straight across the mount (Fig. 85, b) is a hopeful direction for a partnership, often showing islands or breaks in the same place on the hands of both husband and wife, when partings or similar anxieties have been shared.

When a 'Marriage' line (Fig. 85, c) bends down and either elongates itself or joins up with a 'change' line from across the Life Line, the breaking up of the home is threatened by changes over which the subject has no control.

However these lines are only one of the four indications relating to marriage and must be accompanied by at least one of the others when one tries to answer the insistent question of—'Shall I marry?'

1. (Fig. 85, d) The branch off the Life Line on the thumb side of that pathway which we studied with the Life Line (Chapter III, page 165). The ideal Influence Line lies alongside the big one, not so close as to be part of it. This stresses the aspect of home and of someone therein, often picturing adversities endured by the partner and happiness regained.

2. (Fig. 85, e) The Influence Line coming into the Fate Line from the Luna side of the palm. This aspect shows any influence of the partner on the career. Also mentioned under Fate or Duty Line. (Chapter III, page 169).

3. (Fig. 85, f) The cross on the Mount of Jupiter mentioned earlier in this chapter.

While the presence of (1) plus the lines on the Mercury mount suggest every hope of matrimony, any or all of the marks can grow on the palm after marriage when they have not been present before. It is far more important to realize the strength and weakness of one's own and one's partner's hands and to decide in time whether there is compatibility of heart and mind.

Children (Fig. 85, g)

The late Mrs. Linton Wilson spent many years trying to establish the reliability of any indications of children on hands. The presence or absence of the little vertical lines through or above the 'Establishment' lines on Mercury proved to be engraved by the way children were thought about, and not by the number of children born or intended.

(a). For example, people interested in numbers of children such as school teachers, people who had children in the holidays whose parents were abroad, very devoted aunts, all could show a row of a dozen or more little vertical lines; devoted aunt continuing hers all her life. Women who handed over the babies to the care of a nurse and were not greatly interested in their children, showed none. Men do not indicate children with the same facility as women but devoted fathers show them in great detail, especially when there is a favourite whose representing line rises higher, even onto the base of the little finger.

(b). The longer and clearer the line the more pride in the child; and in such a case refer back to the lines parallel to the Life Line on the Mount of Venus (Chapter III, page 165).

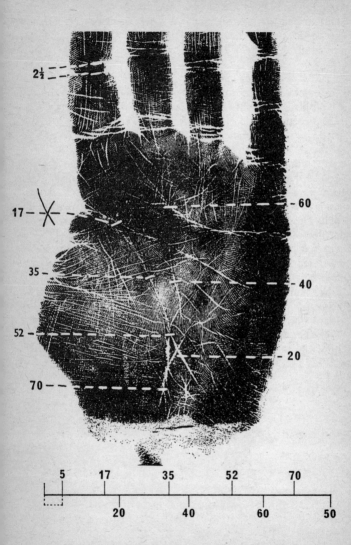

Fig. 86— Print marked for time. Note Ulna loop

CHAPTER V

TIME

T I M E I S one of the most difficult parts of hand interpretation and the subject of incessant argument. This is partly because in this century people old enough to have some history to check, have lived such eventful lives that they can supply a happening for almost any year one mentions. The Life and Fate Lines are the only ones I trust. When the Fate Line is transformed into a Sun Line and veers towards the third finger, the measurement of time may be continued.

The Life Line from its commencement under the first finger right round the thumb till the end of the skin pattern there may be counted as one hundred years. This usually brings the age of seventy to the ridge across the 'heel' of the palm or the base of a print when the hand has just been placed on the paper on a hard surface. I do *not* follow variations in the spacing of the years but divide the distance neatly into halves, quarters, etc.

When the full length that one is going to work from, i.e. either the 70 or the 100 distance is measured, draw a line beneath the print and mark it off with the finest tipped pencil available. When the length is re-measured for half-way, thirty-five, that point will be found under the middle of the Medius finger. Half that again will be found under the Jupiter finger beyond the centre (ten years old or the 'eleven-plus' time is just short of the middle of the Index finger). From the thirty-five mark the same distance as seventeen on one side finds fifty-two on the other.

Having marked these points very lightly in pencil on the

print one next checks with the Fate line. The whole length
from skin pattern beneath Neptune to the joining on of the
Saturn finger is, in a square hand, eighty years. On a long hand
it can represent more years but I have never found it beyond
ninety.

Now take the measurement and put a second lot of dots
on the line beneath the print. I put Life Line above and Fate
Line below. If they coincide one feels safe in dividing the
distance on the print into forty at half-way and, starting from
the wrist end, divide again into twenty and then ten and thirty.
When the ten years is the same place for the dots above and
below there is still another way of checking for which the
S.S.P.P. is indebted to Mir Bashir. When the lower joint of
Index or Medius has three lines across, the space between the
lower two may be the gauge for two and a half years. Not all
fingers have three lines but when they have and the space
goes into the ten year period four times as it should, the result
is most satisfactory.

The Life Line is the more important and I support it against
the Fate Line if there is much divergence but when the three
lines on the Index are present I follow whichever line they agree
with.

The Head Line being so variable in its position on the palm
I cannot subscribe to the theory that the crossing of Fate
and Head is thirty-five years, and the idea is particularly
misleading when the left and right hands cross at different
distances from the wrist. Neither do I agree that the fifteen
busiest years of one's worldly life, i.e. thirty-five to fifty, can
be concentrated between the two transverse lines of Head and
Heart.

There is some difficulty in reading the end of the Life Line
when a thumb is very much turned towards the palm, opposing the fingers, because the actual skin pattern is apt to become
blurred but the diamond, 'elephant hide' back of the hand
skin shows its own line. When one watches for a few moments,
the lines round the Mount of Venus *may* show the true
boundary.

Having made the survey, events shown on Life Line and
on Fate may inspire a discreet question. When both lines show

lands: 'Did you do something foolish at . . . years?' Or—
did you achieve a complete break at thirty-two? That main
incident will correct the measurements and one can proceed
safely from there.

Cheiro had a method of taking lines from the apex of the
Mount of Venus, radially to the apices under the fingers, and
from their crossing of the longitudinal lines, finding Time.
He was wonderful at Time, so any method he used is worthy
of study; though he also checked by Astrology and Numerology in his prognostications. One main difficulty of this
method is in finding the exact apex on the Thenar Eminence,
such a small difference alters all the angles, and when the
Venus grooves have only a faint arched pattern that exact
spot is almost impossible to decide.

Having found the gauge of Time to some degree of satisfaction remember once again that lines can change. Be constructive and see if and how any troubles can be averted;
and above all *never* tell anyone that they will die at X years.
You do not *know* and you are only putting the idea into their
subconscious.

Time was when we thought the Fate Line was quite accurate
and reliable but a brief study of some Tristan da Cunha
hands caused doubts. In one set of prints a major break shows
correctly at forty-three years, but on another twenty-five-year-
old hand, there was no break until in the same area between
Head and Heart. Of course the young owner may decide to
return to England when he is about forty, but the dangers of
prognostication are reinforced.

Another problem is that when we study signs of ill-health
certain areas of the palm refer to organs and are impervious to
Time.

PART FOUR

*

CHIROLOGY AND ANATOMY

CHAPTER I

CHIROLOGY AND ANATOMY

PALMISTS ARE frequently derided for having no scientific theory as a basis for their hypotheses. This Chapter is intended to go at least some way towards remedying this defect.

In a subject so beset with prejudices and inhibitions it would be well to muster recognized physical facts, and see how far tradition rests upon a sure foundation. People, when confronted with chirological statements, often demand some knowledge other than the palmist's upon which they can build an acceptance. Dr. Charlotte Wolff in her book *The Human Hand* made great strides towards fulfilling this need; she relates hands to the cerebral cortex, and to the two main nerves which connect them. This Chapter attempts to go a little further with these connections.

No great idea is entirely true to its conception when men have added to it the dogmas of their own weaknesses and prejudices, be the idea religious, political, economic or hand interpretation. We must ever try to seek the basic unprejudiced truth. The problem also shows in the divergence of language.

The Anatomist and the Chirologist must both allow for the fact that they are using different terminologies. It is immaterial whether one uses the names of Gods of Rome or other Latin words preceded by the name of a modern discoverer. The frequently quoted Heron-Allen,* who translated the writings of Desbarolles (1801-86), the father of modern palmistry, was studying and writing during the period when Sir Charles Bell

* *A Manual of the Science of Chiromancy*

published *The Hand; Its Mechanisms and Vital Endowment as Evincing Design* in 1833.* Both Heron-Allen and Si Charles Bell searched for truth among the traditions, as far a their knowledge would permit; both did good work for thei respective sciences, and both equally deserve credit for th foundations they laid. All the information on Anatomy an Physiology in this work has been checked, or is quoted from Professor Frederick Wood Jones's classic: *The Principles o Anatomy as Seen in the Hand*. Chapter and page reference are to the edition published in 1946. It must be understood that this particular Chapter is written in a spirit of respec and gratitude to the Professor.

Professor Wood Jones is in obvious agreement with palm ists in regarding the hand as the most responsive and expressiv part of the human body. When one considers the intricat design of substitution which enables the hand to work despit injury, our view seems to be well supported by Nature.

Chapter I, Page 5:

The hand as the expressor of emotional states affords a study in itself; it is a study that the physician cannot afford to neglect ...

Chapter XXV, Pages 306-7:

It is notable that in the human brain the large hand area is situated immediately adjacent to the older area in which sensa- tions and movements of the face are represented.

Professor Wood Jones then traces the sequence of cortica representation, continuing:

We may therefore imagine that when once the testing hand and the eye had obtained their large share of cortical grey matter they were the instruments by which the knowledge of the rest of the body as a moving thing became added to the cortex . . . More than this it has caused the whole mechanism for initiating these pictured movements to become entirely cortical, and the functions of the corpus striatum as a motor nucleus are lost in Man.

We may therefore say that not only has the hand an extraordi- narily large share of cortical representation, but it has been a pioneer in leading to the representation of other parts of the body.

---

* Bridgewater Treatises (No. IV).

Chapter XXVII, Pages 328-9:

There are many curious circumstances brought about by abnormal and emotional conditions that clearly give us a hint that in considering the pathology of the hand we must always have regard to the fact that it is no ordinary member, but is a specialized portion of the sensory side of the nervous system which may manifest changes only to be explained by the fact that it is our dominant organ of tactile sensibility.

These quotations very definitely answer the query of why the hand should be especially worthy of study. They bring us to another point of agreement: the importance of the thumb and first finger in the assessment of a human being as a fully representative specimen of the human race.

Another point of agreement between the Anatomist and the Chirologist which must be appreciated from the start is the infinite diversity of hands. One might expect to find each hand having identical muscles, nerves, blood vessels, etc., but over and over again in each Chapter of Professor Wood Jones' book possibility of variation is stressed, of course within general limits of origin and destination (i.e. the main vessels pass through the wrist. Muscles and tendons are attached to bones, and perform the same duties, but vary to a surprising degree in their manner of performance). The anatomist does not yet ally variations with character—as we do—but the physical scope of these variations cannot be dismissed. Hands are not alike.

Most books of reference on the brain written since the publication in 1918 of the work of Sir Henry Head during the First World War present the brain in a diagram resembling the side-view of a walnut. The diagram (Fig. 57, page 130) shows a cleft approximately over the ear, named the 'fissure of Rolando' or post central gyrus. Across it one finds inscribed from ear to crown: Face; Digits (1, 2, 3, 4, and 5); Arm; Trunk, etc; and Leg, which is represented in the brain just under the hair. The diagram shows the area of 'cortical representation' of each part of the body; we can see that the portion of the brain taken up by the hand is very large, and realize how important that member is. But besides revolutionizing brain surgery, Head—unwittingly—revolutionized chirology

G

also. At all events, his works provided our science with a basis of physical fact which proved to correlate with the basis founded on observation only.

To make this knowledge vivid, personal, let us think what it actually means. A rabbit can run and play without the part of the brain that human beings have developed to the present stage. Orders for the rabbit's movements are sent to its body directly from a part at the back of its brain, called the *Corpus Striatum*, in direct response to messages coming in. (Its movement control is, so to speak, short-circuited.) That is why rabbits come out again without any worries directly after the fox has collected his lunch; they cannot picture his return, nor their own place in his next course. Dogs are said to show a further step in cortical representation. They start their movements instinctively, but the cortex is aware of them and can picture them in order to repeat them when required. The training of the puppy, for instance, consists of educating his instinct, his *Corpus Striatum*, to tell his nerves to obey cortical orders in future.

We can see any baby becoming aware of its own thumb and the use of its hands for gesticulation; using the first finger to express a wish by pointing. To the pre-glacial, earliest discovered man, finding that he could sharpen flints by holding them between his thumb and forefinger, must have been a definite step forward. Then he must have become aware of his responsibilities, put the wife and family into a cave, and signalled his complete departure from the ways of his cousins the monkeys and apes by that sensation, that awareness of owning a cave, a family, and a place among other men: in sum, a background which is the idea behind the various interpretations of the second finger today.

What physical justification is there for stressing stability as a characteristic quality of the second finger? It has been described as 'the balance wheel' of the hand; as representing contact with the mundane world, the philosophy of religion, mining, farming, property: in fact, 'background' in its various manifestations. It is noteworthy that people deprived of 'background' by birth or some upheaval in life tend to be, or become, unstable politically, mentally or emotionally.

Anatomy tells us that the metacarpal bone of the Second Finger (third digit) is based on, and deeply slotted with, the 'os magnum' (the biggest bone in the wrist), to which it is firmly bound by ligaments. In a normal human hand, this Second Finger is always the longest. It is the first to ossify in the embryo. The muscles are arranged so that the other fingers spread from it and close on it, for it alone has no short 'interosseous' muscle on the palmar side to move it at the knuckle joint (try to move the second finger when it is bent), although it has a muscle at the back, to move it when extended. The Second Finger shares the Median nerve with the Index Finger and Thumb. As Dr. Wolff pointed out, it is given a share of responsibility for our knowledge of contact with the outer world.

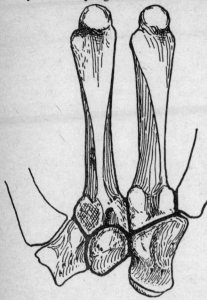

Fig. 87—The method of articulation of the second and third metacarpals with the carpus. Dorsal aspect of right hand. (Wood Jones: *The Principles of Anatomy as seen in the Hand*, Baillière, Tindall & Cassell.)

In order to bend, the Second Finger takes a branch from a tendon shared with the Third Finger (flexor digitorum sublimis and flexor profundus). The finger of Saturn has one other stabilizing task. It serves as a fulcrum to the Thumb. To sum up, bones, muscles, tendons and nerves of the central digit are all designed to ensure fixity. To its metacarpal bone are fastened many of those short muscles which give the Thumb its freedom of movement. In very fact, the stability of the contact with the world allows the freedom of the will.

The Index Finger (of Jupiter)

This finger represents our idea of ourselves in relation to the world of other people. Physical correlation is ample; the first finger appears to be the only specialization Man has developed since the primitive being who lived in London Clay and Thanet Sands in the Eocene period. Some of those skeletons show independent thumb formation, but the development of the finger of Jupiter belongs to our own type of human.

The wrist-bone on which the finger rests is the last to ossify in a baby's wrist; it is therefore assumed to be the last to be developed to its present special shape. This metacarpal bone may be of any length proportionately to the others, in man or monkey, but in man it is always a stout, strong bone. The finger served by this bone is never as long as the third finger in any animal but Man, whose First and Third fingers tend to be level. When the Index is the longer it is usually more pointed than the Second and Third, and 'practically always accompanied by a well-developed and more or less 'expressive' thumb. This type of hand is definitely non-simian, and it constitutes a characteristic human specialization.'*

The tendons which straighten and bend the wrist have a separate attachment to the metacarpal bone of the first finger; the muscle which bends the finger comes into the wrist at a lower level with special tendons for the Index and the little finger. The muscle that straightens it on the back of the hand (extensor digitorum profundus) has been lost to the other fingers but retained by Index and Thumb to give them the power to bend backwards. Man has developed his First Finger as his most treasured birthright. The Index, it will be remembered, is served by the Median nerve, the nerve which is described as having taken over sensation, knowledge of the world, and of our own bodies, from the snout-area of the nose-first animals; the nerve which is responsible to the conscious brain for all the pictured action of the movement that follows from Man's use of his hands.

* Professor Wood Jones: *Principles of Anatomy as seen in the Hand.*

The hand is the great *sense organ* of the body, and of the hand the Index Finger is regarded as of paramount importance.

The claim that it maps the attitude or realization of ourselves is supported from every angle of anatomical knowledge.

The Thumb

The thumb presents at least three separate problems: Why does its natural position of rotation show whether the will is

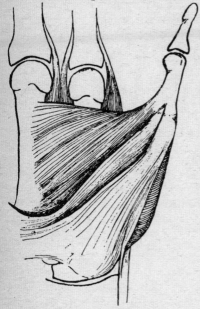

the servant or master of the instincts shown by the fingers? In modern language, why does the angle of rotation of the Thumb represent the degree of inhibition? Why does the nail phalange represent the Will? Why does the base of the Thumb— whether it is included as palm or thumb is immaterial — represent the degree of vitality by its development?

The Thumb is controlled up the back by sors pollicis longus, a long muscle (extenbrevis and proprius) which has almost disappeared in man and now remains only in four tendons of which the Thumb claims three. Attached to the nail phalange it controls the bending back at the joint; another branch draws the Thumb back to alignment with the fingers.

Fig. 88—The superficial view of the intrinsic muscles of the thumb. The adductor, flexor brevis and abductor are in order from above downwards; the opponens is at the extreme radial margin. (Wood Jones: *The Principles of Anatomy as seen in the Hand*, Baillière, Tindall & Cassell.)

This extensor muscle is opposed by short muscles which

arise from Nature's wrist-strap of ligament around the wrist-bones, from the bones of the wrist themselves, and from the metacarpal bone of the Saturn finger (the area of stability).

Is it too fanciful to see the natural position of the Thumb as the picture of our individual balance between the responsibilities which came with the cortical representation of the Second Finger and the freedom of instinct experienced when we were aware only of our thumbs?

The same growth which allowed the development of the extensor pollicis longus into the extreme extent of flexibility of the Thumb at its highest joint might also have coincided with the necessity to quickly grasp the unusual; the alert application of decision which would belong to the same era of evolution. The stiff, persistent Thumb controlling its atavistic tendon is a human evolution.

An interesting example of the truth of this hypothesis was seen in Kenya. Members of the large Asian community had the flexible fingers and thumb usual with the Indian race. Many of the leaders who had undertaken civic and community responsibilities had stiff, European type thumbs without having lost the flexibility of the rest of their hands.

Development of the Mount of Venus is, of course, regulated by the development of the mass of muscle which we have been considering as attached to the metacarpal bone of the Finger of Saturn; but it is also affected by the arteries beneath it. A large mount, showing an excess of vitality, does not necessarily promise a musculary strong thumb, but it invariably shows that Life is strong 'in the veins'. The blood enters the hand at two levels. The upper, Ulnar artery, enters somewhere about the line of the Ring finger; sends strong branches to Mercury and *between all the fingers* to the 'web' where the branches divide to go up the tips. One branch goes to Index, and one to the lower phalange of the Thumb, under which it is usually joined by a branch from one of the other two arteries, Radial or Median, thus forming the 'Superficial Palmar Arch'. It is, however, stressed very strongly that the arrangement has infinite variety from hand to hand.

Under the short muscles, lying upon the cushioned metacarpal bones, is the *Deep* Palmar Arch, formed by the deep-

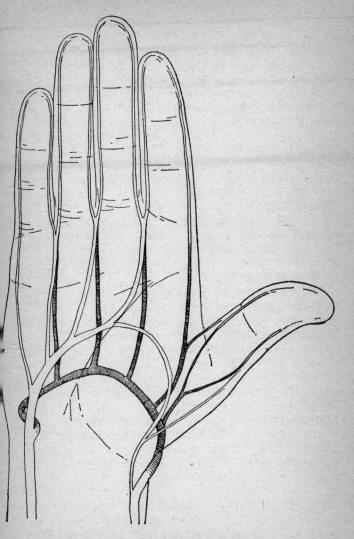

Fig. 89—The deep and superficial palmar arches. (Wood Jones: *The Principles of Anatomy as seen in the Hand*, Baillière, Tindall & Cassell.)

lying branch of the Ulnar artery meeting the main branch of the Radial artery which has crossed the wrist-bones near enough to the surface for the pulse to be taken and has entered the hand right under the Thumb. This arcade also sends branches to the clefts between the fingers where deep and superficial branches unite to send their tracery up the sides of each finger.

This arrangement gives the Mount of Venus the responsibility of protecting the main blood stream into the hand, and its branches towards each side of the important Index Finger as well as the branches to its own Thumb.

Blood is synonymous with Life. Two arteries, healthy, powerful and protected by walls of healthy fascial padding, will take up appreciably more room than a poor blood supply system, with incomplete superficial arches, and a poor bore to its main deep radial stream. In illness, the possessor of a generous, healthy circulatory system has a better chance of recovery; and in health, a fuller enjoyment of life.

Mount of Mars Positive

Before we leave the Thumb, we must consider the physical basis for the muscular development at the junction of Thumb and Index representing the map of physical courage. The muscle underlying this Mount of Mars is a big abductor (drawing in) mass from the whole length of the metacarpal bone of the Medius Finger, with attachments to Index and an oblique part originating at the wrist, all 'buttoned' to the joint by a little 'Sesamoid' bone and finally attached to the phalange of Reason.

Unlike the lower thumb muscles, these are served by that Ulnar nerve which Dr. Wolff holds responsible for the 'subconscious side of the hand' (Fig. 9, page 24). It might be interesting to note that there seems to be some ground for associating this area with the Adrenal Glands.

The Ring Finger (of Apollo), finger of happiness and the appreciation of beauty, seems to share everything appertaining to it. It shares tendons, blood supply, and nerves; for, as we have seen, both Median and Ulnar serve their respective sides.

This part of the hand represents a transition stage. It has been said that with the cortical representation of the Third Finger, civilization began.

Think of the primitive man with his cave-home and his family responsibilities. It must have been at a very early stage that some son of his, taken out to hunt the reindeer, saw the beauty of their movements, and on his return drew them on the wall. The French caves at Dordogne, and the drawings in our own Somerset caves near Wookey Hole, suggest how long ago this must have been. One can picture the lad (rather in disgrace for not paying attention to the business in hand) with his long Third Finger, probably spatulate, illustrating for the stay-at-homes the beauty he saw and felt. A step had been taken: 'I am' had passed into 'Something I see makes me feel happy'. Expression probably followed quickly on realization.

Little Finger (of Mercury). Independence of muscle, artery and nerve to the little finger, though not as marked as in the Thumb, ranks next to it. Like the Thumb, the little finger has its flexor tendons protected by their own sheath from wrist-band to nail phalange, showing design for freedom of movement, and protection from contact with outer objects. The Fourth Finger usually has three tendons up the back to extend it, two of its own and it may share a slip from the branch of the tendon which activates the Third and Second fingers, but this arrangement again is variable. On the palm the Fourth finger shares the deeper layer of flexor muscle with the First finger. Usually its share is much the lighter of the two: but 'the deep portion of the muscle is liable to considerable minor variations, and hardly any two subjects will show the muscle in exactly similar form' (Professor Wood Jones).

Flexor Sublimis goes to the middle phalange, and its undue strength (or contraction) produces that angulation at the joint which to palmists warns of some kink in the sub-conscious mind. At first glance this may not make sense, but why does that particular tendon contract? We must bear this question in mind when we consider the place of fascial covering in the living hand.

Mount of Mars Negative

Palmists, including Dr. Wolff, say that the hand beneath the finger of Mercury, and onwards to half-way under Apollo, is the map of the sub-conscious mind. Further, they say that the Mount of Luna itself shows the degree of rapport with Nature, inherited memories, etc.

I quote from *The Principles of Anatomy as Seen in the Hand*, by Dr. F. Wood Jones:

> In the palmar fascia, upon the ulnar side of the hand, are somewhat variable muscular fibres, which run at right angles to the long axis of the hand, and are mostly inserted into the deep surface of the skin over the ulnar border of the hand. These muscular fibres produce a puckering of the skin when they contract, and when well developed they are capable of producing a long depression in the skin running from the base of the little finger to the wrist. This muscle—the palmaris brevis—has several distinctions . . . It is a muscle that appears to produce an action which has but little cortical representation, and is therefore one which it is not easy to activate by volition . . .

Dr. Wood Jones then describes how it responds to pressure of the skin by reflex action, but 'the meaning of this reflex awaits solution'. The muscle is absent in monkeys and anthropoid apes, though a form of it is present in marsupials and some lemurs. Dr. Wood Jones thinks it is a protective mechanism, but that although it is a fairly human distinction its utility is not very apparent.

> It is possible that here again we have lingering in Man an extremely primitive muscle which has long since been lost in all those animals so often regarded as his phylogenetic forebears.

Or has Man found it wise to treasure and cultivate this ancient sensing gift when so much of his daily thought is done by his cerebral cortex? For example, a sailor cannot 'think' the weather ahead. Even now, with all the modern instruments, mistakes are often made; but he refers the matter to his latent instinct and senses the coming storm. Navigators always have this part of the hand very well developed.

CHAPTER 11

CHIROMANCY IN RELATION TO ANATOMY AND PHYSIOLOGY

> . . . he is the wise physician and philosopher who realizes that in regarding the external appearance of his fellow-men he is studying the external nervous system and not merely the skin and its appendages.
>
> *Principles of Anatomy as Seen in the Hand*: Professor Wood Jones.

How strongly this applies to the hand with its superior quantity of nerve endings, both deep and superficial!

Let us follow the path of a movement initiated by a message from the cortex. We wish to—hold a pencil. We do not 'think', 'flexors sublimis and index profundis contract, extensors, will oppose, X numbers of fibres will be engaged, thumb muscles will . . .', etc. Anyone who has tried to learn golf or to hold reins will know how stupid muscles make themselves when under direct instruction from the conscious Will. They will also know the relief when, having finally shown them what we want we can just say to the ball, not to our body—'proceed to yonder flag'.

This little illustration shows how much of the work of selection, co-ordination and action is performed autonomically. There are a number of 'private paths' for transforming messages into action, while the motor and sensory pathways of the nervous systems are 'wired up' to these pathways. A full description makes the terminal board of an automatic telephone look like a child's toy. Any description will be but a rough sketch of some of the possibilities.

A 'private path' allows the corpus striatum to 'press the right buttons' to ensure a smooth continuous movement, any damage along these 'paths' produces a well-defined tremor. Its 'opposite number' in the sensory, or incoming, track is the thalamus, which retains in addition a good deal of initiative, such as reflexes to pain.

A private path from the cerebellum to the horn cell in the spinal column is responsible for proper co-ordination of movement. It decides which muscles shall be used, and in which capacity. Yet another, called the 'vestibular spinal tract', is responsible for the balance of the movement, the appreciation of, the feel and weight of the pencil and of its position in space. The incoming flow from the sense organs, from the four different types of terminals on the skin surface from three or four types in the dermis, and yet again from a deep layer containing at least four more types, all streaming their reports up the lines to the spinal cord, could not possibly be dealt with by any act of consciousness. On the way, in a truly wonderful manner, they sort themselves into pain, touch, heat, cold, etc. Pain reports to the thalamus, which has the power of forwarding a message to the cortex, and of short-circuiting a message to the motor nerves to take action. A large proportion of the pathways of sensibility, especially deep sensibility, go directly to the cerebellum, which is one of the mechanisms forming the intermediaries between deep sensibility and movement. It regulates the poise of moving parts and co-ordinates the impulses connected with muscle sense, and the tone necessary to effect balance and posture.

When the motor part of the cortex is destroyed, a man cannot perform a pictured action, but the required muscles may work as part of the team to yawn or withdraw from pain. In this case the muscles of the hand do not wither though the lines tend to change. When the sensory part of the cortex is destroyed, man is not deprived of the feeling of pain, but he cannot locate it accurately, neither estimate weight, nor recognize the sense of touch.

This picture of activity was borne in mind when we considered the lines on the hand, and the value of unconscious gesture.

Capillary Lines

On the skin pattern of the palm itself we studied the ridges and furrows of the 'Fairy Plough'. These are technically known as capillary lines, and are formed by a thickening below and above skin level to give the necessary resistance on the palm to ensure a precise sensitive hold. Through the thickness of the ridges the sweat glands open in regular series under the control of their sympathetic nerves, and in the furrows alongside are found more nerve endings.

The skin pattern never changes from birth to death; but, following the work of Noel Jaquin, it is proved that before the onset of organic disease part of the pattern disappears as though some of the terminals were no longer alive (see page 252 and Fig. 98, page 228). With returning health the pattern reasserts itself, suggesting very forcibly that much disease is the result of an 'electrical' breakdown and could often be averted were Nature's warning heeded.

Palmists are sure that the patterns found in finger pad and palm are indicative of the natural trend or inclination of thought; certainly the patterns show the 'wiring system' of the hand, and may yet prove to have a correspondence with the 'wiring' plan of the brain. At the moment this idea is pure conjecture. So much work remains to be done on the intricacies of the nervous system.

Cleavage Lines

The 'cleavage lines' of the Anatomist are described as strands of dermal fibrous tissue which make up the skin, thus allowing for the necessary elastic effect. They are to be seen easily in a mesh-like pattern on the back of the hand and around the palmar boundary. They often ray around the 'Family line' of the thumb, especially across the Mount of Mars towards the Index finger, and are to be seen along the line of the fingers in the two lower phalanges. These lines are primarily a health sign, probably related to biochemical deficiencies, and the less they show the better. Everyone knows the look of hands that have been too long in detergent and lost the natural oil. When cleavage lines show in the same manner with no similar cause, it indicates that the skin is being starved of some constituent. For example, in glandular troubles these lines invariably become prominent on the pad, and fade out with returning health thus restoring the finger-print pattern. Sometimes a few lines, or one deep line, will evolve from a cleavage line and remain up a finger, showing that the owner has a burden of awareness about the particular aspect of life represented by that finger. For instance, a strong line up the Index finger shows a burden of awareness of self among other people, conscientiousness. Up the Second finger, as a prolongation of the Fate Line, it shows the restrictions implied by the presence of a strong line of 'fate' driving up into the very being. In normal cases it is very difficult to determine whether these indications are of psychological value. In this category falls the film of barely discernible lines superimposed on the percussion between the Heart and Head Lines in certain conditions of rheumatism. Sometimes one sees in the hands of young people a little 'step-ladder' of extra lines below the Heart Line, under the Third and Fourth fingers. This usually indicates a need for more calcium or silica, etc., but I do not know if the lines are really formed by fibres, or by the heart complaining of its blood supply.

Beneath the Skin

Lines were discussed fully in the Introduction to Part Three, Chapter I. It is therefore helpful to consider the construction of a hand immediately under the skin, and the formation of the mounts which give such value to the lines of awareness.

Directly under the skin is a 'glove' of superficial Fascia which includes the sponge-like fibre mesh retaining the only fat in the hand. An inquirer expects a fat person to have a fat hand, and discounts the thickness through, or the height of the 'mounts' (fleshy eminences) as merely fat. The thickness of the hand is made up of joints, tendons, and short muscles, which do not contain fat. Fat is found solely in this superficial layer and can be recognized easily.

It is important to appreciate the value of this Fascia. Professor Wood Jones describes it as: 'Tissues of low organization which remain undifferentiated when other structures

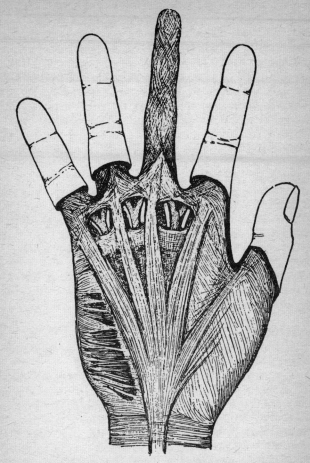

Fig. 90—The fascias of the palm of the hand. (Wood Jones: *The Principles of Anatomy as seen in the Hand*, Baillière, Tindall & Cassell.)

acquire their definite specializations. Fascia . . . may be said to form the packing material of the animal body.'

This glove under the skin has four tendons of an almost obsolete muscle which run from the centre of the wrist to each finger. They must vary very much in development as they are not always even drawn in the same way diagrammatically. They exist habitually, and as the hand is stretched out the lines to the base of each finger often lie upon these tendons. The lines of Sun and Fate go towards the centre of the Third and Second Fingers respectively. The course of the Life Line, after it has emerged from under the Mount of Jupiter, and cleared the short muscles of the digital side of the thumb, often follows the tendon of the first finger. These tendons are described as strongly fibrous, their fibres arranged in a regular manner, and the tissues not woven by strands running in diverse directions. They often present a beautiful pearly sheen of bluish or greenish iridescence. It might well be that it is because they are taut and slippery that the softer padding folds on to them. Was Dr. Benham thinking of these regular fibres of pearly sheen when he envisaged his flow of Life Force on to the hand and thence to the brain?

Across the base of the hand this 'glove' becomes a kind of wrist-strap extending across the wrist-bones, which extend so unexpectedly far into the palm. In other words, the bases of the Mounts of Venus and Luna are formed by ligaments around the further carpal bones and are the origins of the muscles for thumb and Minimus (Fourth Finger).

The ligament 'strap' for the finger end of the metacarpal bones, keeping the fingers in their place at the knuckles, is at a very deep level, next to the bones, so it affects the mounts at the base of the fingers only indirectly. These mounts are formed by the padding which protects the blood vessels where their deep and their superficial layers inter-blend, and prepare to go up the sides of the fingers. Old-fashioned palmists used to expect each fleshy mount to lie exactly under its finger. The description 'displaced' was used when this did not occur.

The independence of the Fourth Finger, Minimus, tends to bring the Mercury Line, when present, to the inner boundary of that finger. Any packing material available will be placed to afford cover to the blood vessels.

Importance of Fascia

The whole thickness and firmness of the hand depends upon

the quality and quantity of this all-pervading fascial covering.

Every nerve is insulated individually; the groups of nerves are bound together, all by fascia.

Every joint has its capsule of fascia to control its articulation and to contain its supply of synovial oil.

Every blood vessel has its covering of fascia.

Every ligament that binds, or tendon that conveys the power of a muscle, is of fascia; where these tendons are designed to withstand the friction of a moving part, or for the inside of a flexing joint, where it runs in a sheath, this is of fascia.

All padding that keeps parts in their proper place, or serves to avert danger from knife or blow, every partition that restricts injury to its own area, is fascia.

This material loses its distinctive elasticity once life has gone, and then it is impossible to appreciate its true value.

Every palmist will agree that well-developed mounts mean life, energy, the power of a strong engine, in whatever part of the hand they occur. In view of their construction they might be seen to work on the same principle as the condensers on the ignition system of a motor car.

CHAPTER III

THE HAND IN PSYCHOLOGICAL ILL-HEALTH

S O   M U C H ill-health is attributed to psychosomatic origin these days that there is sometimes a tendency to dismiss continued poor health to 'nerves'. A study of the hands will often help to clear up the problem of how much is in the mind, how much has attained physical form; and, even more important, how much is incipient trouble sending an appeal for help.

For long years books on palmistry have had a chapter on the medical aspect, but have mostly confined themselves to disfigurements of the actual lines. Nails became recognized after the experience of Dr. Geikie Cobb, the pioneer of research on the Endocrine System, during his attack of pneumonia. Medical knowledge itself has made such strides during the last fifty years that the published prints in the older books suggest different causes and explanations for the very illnesses they illustrate.

The famous Frenchman, M. Henri Mangin, has written two books devoted to the aspects of health and disease. He had an international reputation and did much good work in converting the dubious. One of his greatest interests lay in dividing people into 'types' and then studying where they diverged from the full picture of the type.

Certainly a type-picture is essential as a basis that one may see where divergencies lie; for example, a long sloping Head Line denoting imagination found on a square practical palm or the reverse; a straight Head Line with a message of truth, straight thinking, the no-nonsense attitude, on a long hand with pointed fingers, etc., but, to me, the great value of hand-interpretation lies in the recognition and assessment of the individual. As in all work on hands the influence of health is again divided into shape, including nails, colour and texture; lines with their formation and temporary disruptions; and skin pattern.

However, I propose to divide the study into Psychological and Physical aspects, taking the psychological side first, and including all three approaches in turn.

Finger Patterns

As we saw in Chapter II of Part Two, Arched fingers are rather inarticulate about their own feelings, even to themselves. They like to be doing rather than thinking or talking. The result is that when something in their lives goes terribly wrong, some happening that they cannot *do* anything about, they sometimes may have a nervous breakdown. When they try to fight their way back to health by reading books on psychology they identify themselves with the symptoms described therein. They are questioned as usual, and being instinctively on the defensive they give a personal-sounding resumé of the latest book or theory. The poor doctor-psychiatrist, delighted to have such a clear case, treats in accordance with the text book, with no result whatever. This effect may be seen with just the Index fingers arched, but with a complete, or nearly complete, set the resistance behaviour is vastly increased. If the arches are accompanied by a sloping Head Line it seems impossible for any rope to be long enough to reach the bottom of that well of truth.

These arched people seem the ideal ones for the treatment based on painting or expressing themselves in some form of artistic craftsmanship. Give their sub-conscious free rein by occupying their conscious thoughts and they may reveal that which they do not know themselves.

Whorls

The whorl is another rather closed-in form of pattern. They do not talk of their deeper troubles easily but they usually know themselves and try to mend themselves. A complete set, or even six whorled digits out of the ten, as long as the thumb is included, is so busy finding and occupying its own niche that it can rise above disaster. Difficulties occur when whorled fingers are ruled by composite or one composite and one looped thumb. With every work they try to undertake the double loop is whispering a tale of alternatives and doubt, and generally hindering the whorled fingers in their urge to help the world. Then, annoyed with their own dalliance, the owners of such hands become irritable, ashamed of being unhappy in themselves, and many even try to retire into their own corner, hating themselves because of the unworthiness of the niche they did not select.

When the companion thumb to the composite is whorled the partnership seems to make for slower decisions but, with patience, the whorl seems able to dominate the difficult pattern. Two looped thumbs with whorled fingers have the gift of adapting their owners to work with other people as long as they have developed enough will power to get started. They often say that their work is perhaps not quite what they would have chosen, but they find it interesting and make the best of wherever they find themselves.

Often slightly out-of-tune whorls are helped by seeing the conflict in their hands and understanding that their patterns can be used as a gift in that, unlike full whorls, they can see both sides of a question, so their ultimate judgement will be better balanced. One of the arts of a happy life is to see one's attributes as gifts, not curses. The idea is far better expressed by Dr. Graham Howe in his theory of 'acceptance'.

Loops

Looped fingers do not seem to have their psychological problems woven into their fabric. They may have as many troubles as anyone else but their conflicts are more likely to appear with their lines; they can see and express their feelings and will be likely to accept the rules of treatment leading to recovery.

Tented Arches

Of tented arches I have had no experience, those I have

met have been far too busy putting the world to right to bother about their own conflicts. There may be quite different findings in a mental hospital.

Palmar Patterns

As we noted in the study of patterns in Chapter V, Part Two, Dr. Debrunner states that a frequent sign of schizophrenia is found in whorl patterns on the mount of the percussion, the Hypothenar Eminence (or Luna). This, it must be repeated, does *not* mean that everyone with a whorled Mount of Luna is schizophrenic, but people who suffer from this complaint usually have this pattern—which is quite a different rule. To reason out the premise, the mount of the Hypothenar is the part of the hand definitely related to the subconscious (there is even a muscle with no direct connection with the brain). A whorl is the sign of individualism, so the presence of a whorl should, and will, individualize the hidden self. This individualization of the hidden self may be used in many ways; in 'good works' it produces the extra sympathy of, 'There, but for the grace of God, go I.' The whorl has been found on the hands of people who go to the pictures and dream all night of being the hero or heroine in dire distress. When the Head Line runs into this pattern there may well be wonderful expression in writing, reporting, or portraiture.

Composite

A composite pattern is infrequent on the Hypothenar Eminence but not rare. In this Lunarian position it retains the duality. I have met people who foster a mistrust of their own intuitive gifts, and I have seen flexibility of the second joint of the Medius finger (too easily self-persuaded) with the entwined loops, but have not enough examples to do more than suggest a future line of inquiry. The duality of outlook should be explained to the owners that they may understand and use the pattern constructively, as when the form appears on the fingers.

Ulna Loop

As we saw in Part II, Chapter V, pages 121 and 122, and

Fig. 86, page 184, the Ulna loop on the Mount of Luna has been found by Dr. Debrunner, the Galton Laboratory, Dr. Wolff, and in the U.S.A. on the hands of eighty per cent of mongoloids.

This pattern is not confined to this form of mental distress, as a very large proportion of the British Society of Dowsers show the Ulna loop on at least one of their hands.

When I suggested to Dr. Debrunner that we had found the loop connected with an instinctive feeling for the radiations of Móther Earth he agreed, telling me that he found the mongoloid patients were happy and successful on farms and in horticulture. Kipling's Bee Boy* comes to mind as the pictured representative of the affliction.

Strictly, the condition of mongolism is physical manifestation, but since the affliction is studied by the psychiatric branch of medicine I have included the pattern in this chapter.

The transverse lines are frequently distorted into either one 'simian' line across the palm or a broken, unconnected Head Line, but any reader especially interested should read Dr. Wolff's books. Fig. 68, page 148 is not Mongoloid though a pronounced 'simian'.

Deterioration of Lines

All books on hand interpretation observe and comment on little dark dots on and little cuts across the main lines but many theories of exact location do not appear infallible. A dot in one place does not always mean a pain in a corresponding spot in or on the body, though it may do so. To find the basic, underlying meaning one must remember that the body is full of streams and canals, fluid flowing through arterial, venous and lymphatic systems and, above all, that the brain is kept alive and fed by a wondrous, intricate canal system.

When there are little dark dots on the transverse lines of Head and Heart they suggest tensions or worry impeding the natural flow. These dots are essentially of the mind and it is safe to picture them as registering that some nerves, or groups of nerves, probably in the autonomic nervous system, are impeding the flow and will, unless corrected, lead to breakdown of the physical health at any weak link. I find these dots a sure

* Rewards and Fairies

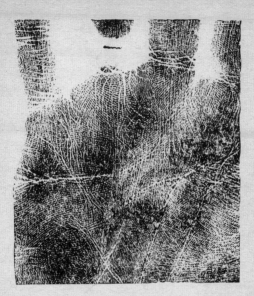

Fig. 91—Dots and cuts led to inexplicable deterioration in health. Also lines too fine

sign of mental stress causing ill-health.

Little cuts across the line tell much the same story but it is possible that they register more of a feeling of being thwarted over their attempts to do what they want, rather than an inner tension. The difference is very subtle and may not always be an accurate distinction, but I expect dots to show inner tensions especially of fear, and the cuts to show more outside worries. However the important root of the matter lies in the probability of any physical discomforts being caused by anxiety.

A 'rule of thumb' hypothesis, not yet fully proven, is that blemishes on the Head Line relate to one's personal worries, whereas the same markings on the Heart Line refer to one's worries about other people.

Fig. 92—Left and right hands of same architect. Note differences in Transverse lines, patterns on Hypothenar, etc.

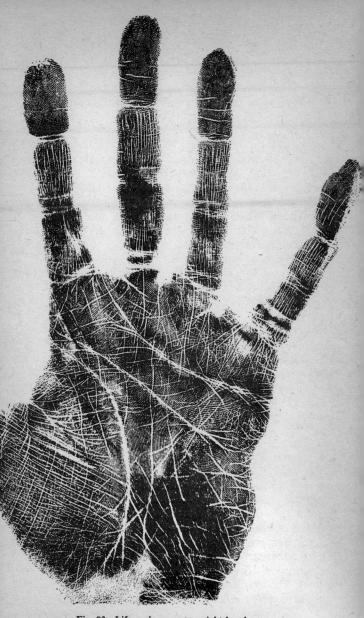

Fig. 93—Life-saving cross on right hand

An ordinary, straightforward worry which is not likely to affect the delicate balance of health is shown by a line becoming islanded, i.e. splitting into two and rejoining, but this phenomenon really belongs to the next chapter.

Depth

A very fine, deeply engraved line of Head and/or Life sometimes found on a well-padded hand, can also be a source of tension. The characteristic of such a fine clean line is singleness of purpose. When it appears to be deeply engraved the picture is of too great a tenseness, of single-mindedness. This type of line becomes over-tired all too easily but drives on refusing to rest until rest can no longer be achieved. I always beg the owners to knock off for a cup of tea, a cigarette, a walk-about, anything to ease the tension, promising them that when work is resumed the brain will work more easily again. But, when driven beyond the power to recuperate, there will appear that conscientious to neurotic person who feels there is no hope of easing off, though the half is not really necessary.

An entanglement of many, fairly indefinite lines shows a highly sensitive nervous system. The message is of great value when seen on the hands of an outwardly placid person. Trust the implication of the tracery and not the outward appearance should physical manifestations occur.

Conflicts

The shape of a hand in relation to the lines often shows the grounds for a recognizable 'conflict'; though perhaps the most obvious cause occurs when the right and left hands are very different (Figs. 92 and 93). There may be found the history of parents having a completely differing attitude to life and the child inheriting one parent on one hand and the other parent on the other hand.

I do not suggest that all inheritors of mixed parentage show this peculiarity, but when the divergence is present between the hands the meaning may be sought in the parents or grand-parents. Though Galton could not satisfy himself that different races bore clearly differentiated hand prints, this right and left disparity often shows up clearly when the parents have been racially different. To the owners the unexpected traits of character can be very upsetting; they do not understand themselves and seek help. When the cause is explained and they can recognize a bit of, say, grandfather coming out they can laugh *with* themselves at seeing the likeness.

Another frequent source of conflict is found with ultra-pointed fingers. These people are the dreamers, the people with ideas, not naturally the Do-ers, but their dreams can be so vivid in their minds that they expect results before they have really started the selected task; they also find it difficult to stay with one task long enough to achieve the dream. The effect is increased when pointed fingers are teamed with a long, sloping Head Line giving imagination, or a very flexible thumb showing quick but unstabilized will power, or both. A straight Head Line, seeking the truth, will present a hard path with the two sides of the nature at war; but the combination, once taught to work in harmony, is useful for achievement.

Sometimes a 'barbed wire entanglement' of lines may be present with either of these conditions and shows the strain on the nervous system.

When pointed fingers are found on white, pudgy, small hands with small ineffective looking thumbs there can be a real physical illness such as diabetes, arthritis or angina which never responds fully to treatment. With such hands I suspect a basic allergy to work, to facing the world of competition and struggle. As a chirologist one can only seek some creative gift which could give these people an interest in life. If anyone can find the right chord they may go through life as patient invalids, happily creating beautiful embroidery, until well past their eightieth birthday. But spare a sympathetic and helpful thought for the relatives of the mollusc and do not get impatient with them that they cannot break free. The mollusc instinct guides it to the safest rock.

Childhood Traumas

Childhood experiences are often blamed for adult difficulties. A study of the hand is most useful to decide whether the trouble is from childhood, from a difficult task in life, as shown by the skin pattern, from lack of courage or determination, or just from an inflated ego.

Disasters which have left their mark are memorized in the line pattern from the edge of the palmar boundary at the side of the Index finger, on the Life Line as it passes under the first finger. Stars, crosses, islands and breaks will relate to unhappy childhood memories, while little lines rising towards the mount, show the memory of efforts to conquer difficulties. Little lines down towards the thumb show an appeal to courage and might reappear as some reserve or resentment in adult life. Upward lines hold the feeling of success.

A slightly frayed effect is quite a normal beginning.

Fig. 94—Fear of mother
Note line between stars

Fig. 95—Loss of parents when very young

Thumb

A very close held thumb suggests tensions and inhibitions which may be attributed to early training and sometimes is confirmed by too deeply engraved lines.

This tightly held thumb is a signal of habitual over-tension which may well lead to illness unless the cause of the tension can be removed. The warning is in the habitual closeness, lack of space between thumb and index when the hand is opened as distinguished from the freely opening thumb which yet faces the fingers, showing the will controlling instinctive thought. Here we have freedom of the soul, not inhibitions.

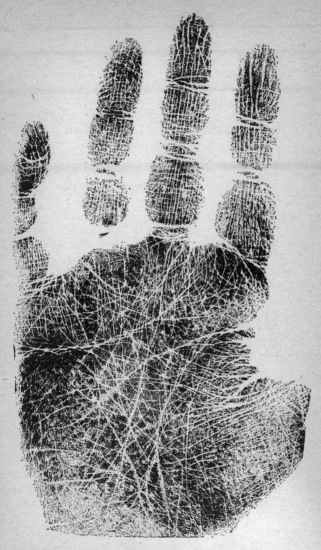

Fig. 96—After shock treatment. Note effect on endocrine system

Lines across Nail Phalanges

Some years ago the late Mr. Cherrill when Head of the Finger Print Department at Scotland Yard wrote to *Nature* about lines he had noticed across the finger prints of criminals which he named 'White Lines' and observed especially on the left hands. The S.S.P.P. took up the challenge and studied many, many examples on ordinary hands. We had found a close relation between lines on finger prints and the endocrine system, we then found that the 'White Lines' always followed a period of frustration, not infrequently affecting the glandular health.

We therefore submit the hypothesis that lines *across* the finger show the respective gland upset by emotional frustration. This would be in accord with the frequent presence of this peculiarity on the hands of Mr. Cherrill's prisoners. (See Figs. 93, page 217 and 102, page 238.)

A further proof of the close alliance of hand and brain is shown in Fig. 96 as the effect E.S.T. (electric shock treatment). Each line of the 'barbed wire entanglement' has the little white star of shock. This is an extreme case on a naturally sensitive hand, but the library holds other examples when mental shocks have been constantly repeated between periods of acute anxiety. The deep lines up the finger pads show that the endocrine system is involved as well.

The prints of people after such treatment might be a useful field of investigation into the exact location of the areas of the hand in connection with the organs.

CHAPTER IV

THE HAND IN PHYSICAL ILL-HEALTH

THERE IS a wealth of information in old and classic books on the subject of Medical Palmistry but since the tremendous strides in medical knowledge, during the last years, most of the deductions are now obsolete and need reassessment.

When one does not know where to begin to look it is only human to put off the effort of looking. This chapter is a suggestion for a sure foundation from which the search may begin; all statements have a backing of examples from the Library of the S.S.P.P.

The two really valuable writers on the health aspect are Noel Jaquin and Dr. Charlotte Wolff. As long ago as 1823 Purkenje commented on a breakdown of the skin pattern. Galton observed the condition also, but not until Noel Jaquin's work with his doctor friends was the breaking up of the rhythm of ridges definitely connected with the warning of disease. His book *The Hand Speaks* has probably the best illustrations of his findings.

Dr. Wolff has based her work on her exhaustive study of backward and mongoloid children and adults. She deals primarily with the psychological side, but as one studies her illustrative prints one finds oneself asking *why* these people are suffering ill-health. Dr. Wolff blames the endocrine system in many cases but that only puts the 'why' a little further along the path. So often some of the answer is shown by a fuller study of the prints.

Noel Jaquin maintains that in all cases of constitutional

troubles, cancer, tuberculosis, forms of the rheumatic family, etc., there is a definite breaking up of the ridges of the skin long before any physical manifestation. The pattern, it will be remembered, is formed by literally thousands of nerve endings, and when the pattern disintegrates certain 'circuits' appear to have been cut out so that they no longer function.

The cause of the failure of these circuits may be due to faults of the endocrine system as many pioneers contend that a perfect glandular system does not, for instance, allow cancer. The failure may be due to tenseness in the autonomic nervous system, or some form of poisoning by bacteria, poison, or mineral imbalance.

The disintegration of the skin pattern is best seen through a magnifying glass. With a very fine skin a print is essential; or rather several prints taken at the same time, as the tightening of a muscle may smudge an area, or heat from the hand produce blobs. Two good prints taken at the same time are wiser for such delicate observation. With prints one can also see, by comparison with another taken after a suitable interval, whether, as the result of sublimating the worry, wise medical treatment, or diet, the pattern is beginning to resume the normal conformation or is not responding to care.

Always make sure that no outside effect, such as a tool or implement of sport, has been rubbing on one area of skin without being enough to produce a noticeable hardening. Should any of the breaking up signs be found they are not an inevitable signal of dire prognostications. For the layman I suggest asking one's ailing friends to allow a print to be taken for research when their medical advisers have diagnosed. Should one find bad signs on the hands of a seemingly fit person one can often inquire, as a matter of friendly interest, how is the . . . digestion? Or whatever the hand may have suggested. Often one then listens to a tale of woe and has to make suitable, sensible suggestions but taking the greatest care not to alarm the owner in any way.

Having observed the faulting of ridges they can be related to the area of the hand. The problem to the Chirologist arises when someone complains of feeling out of sorts but medical examination has revealed no positive cause; yet, upon the hand

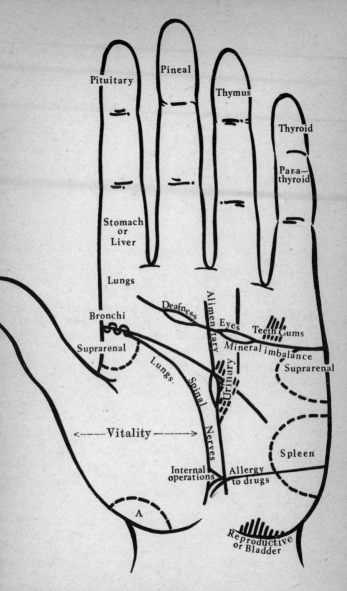

Fig. 97—Areas of location

may be found an indication that the subject is not just suffering from imaginative nerves but has had the amber light of early warning in time to be restored to full health if taken seriously.

Areas of Location

There is a sad lack of agreement on the exact location of the various organs on the palmar surface and more work remains to be done by a careful study of prints. I received my first 'map' from Mrs. Barraclough, the eminent Radiesthetist but have only mentioned those areas which can be supported by, at least, several prints.

Fingers

Starting at the finger prints, on the nail phalanges we see the correspondence with the endocrine sytem. Little lines and veiling appearing in the length of the finger show the gland protesting about some physical discomfort. (Fig. 96, page 221).

Many prints show the connection of the Little finger with the Thyroid Gland. We cannot yet prove whether it is under- or overworking as both extremes show little lines rising from the joint and eventually covering the whole finger print, so that one can no longer be certain of the ridge pattern. There is a suggestion that the Thyroid only overworks when trying to compensate for a lazy Pituitary, which may explain the difficulty in differentiation. The intrusive lines just register a protest.

Some of the Members of the S.S.P.P. suggest the hypothesis that the Para-thyroid registers on the middle phalange of the Little finger, but they have not yet produced enough prints for inclusion in this chapter.

Ring Finger

The Ring Finger is in communion with the Thymus Gland. Observation of this lining or veiling may be useful in determining the cause of erratic blood pressure when the actual circulatory systems seem to be in order and an apparently sound heart is yet suspect.

The Medius Finger

We suggest that the middle finger is one of the places in sympathy with the Pineal Gland and responsible, with the spleen, for the intake and ingestion of the cosmic radiation which flows through all life. I have found people, too easily affected by undue fall-out, to show a halo of little lines around the tip of that finger but we would be grateful for comment by people subject to such radiation.

The 'Earth' end of the connection appears to be on the Mount of Neptune in the middle of the wrist boundary. (In Chapter II, Part One, page 27, we saw how a development of this area indicated extra vitality or magnetism).

The Index Finger

The Index finger is responsible for the pituitary gland which also seems to be shown at the lower angle of the thumb. We have only had a few cases of definite pituitary imbalance but a marked cluster of little lines showed at the wrist in addition to the marks of the first finger (Fig. 97, a).

The Thumb

The Thumb rules all. The print does not seem to relate to any specific gland. Personally I relate the nail phalange of the thumb to our Cosmic Vitality. If one believes that there is a divine spark in each of us then the thumb pictures the health of that 'at-one-ness' and when people are frustrated, unhappy, out of tune with themselves and life the thumb becomes lined, usually with the cross frustration lines we saw in the last chapter. This reading is my own hypothesis which I submit for further investigation.

Lower Phalanges

Some inquirers have suggested that the liver and stomach are represented on the base phalanges of the first finger, one on each hand according to sex and right-handedness. These sections are still a very closed book. The sense of taste is certainly found on this section but one judges more by height and size rather than skin or linear markings.

The Palm

Extending down the palm for the full width of the second finger, for about two-thirds of the length of the hand towards the wrist, (Fig. 97) is the location in sympathy with the alimentary track. Any breakdown of the pattern in this area beneath the Medius finger warns of digestive troubles. With a

Fig. 98—Area affected by removal of kidney

marked disruption of pattern any such difficulty should be investigated that the threat may be averted in time.

Using the third finger in a similar manner as a gauge of width, any breakdown of skin ridges or veiling by little superficial lines resembling the flames of a fire, will draw attention to the urinary system. The flame effect will sometimes rise from a Fate or Sun Line and dance upwards to cross the Head Line.

This signal under the third finger sometimes appears as a corollary to other indications of acidity or digestive troubles and mirrors the complaints of the kidneys about the extra work. I have various prints of people who have had kidney troubles and two prints of people who have lost one kidney and they all show the skin pattern and flame effect as in Fig. 98.

There is one area which can be confirmed in all too many hands—it lies between the two horizontal lines on the percussion side of the palm (Fig. 99). At first the skin pattern does

not disintegrate dramatically but becomes covered with many fine upright lines; these become crossed and interwoven into a typical veiling which shows that the Suprarenal Glands are not working properly and warns of that type of chronic rheumatic complaints that respond to cortisone. The condition suggests that some form of poisoning, which includes acidity, is the cause of the breakdown of the gland; or, malfunction of the gland is allowing poison into the system. The veiling can disappear in the course of a few weeks when the cause is found and corrected. (See also Chapter V, Silica.)

Fig. 99—Early warning of rheumatic ailment

There is probably a distinction between the Cortex and the Medulla as the picture appears on the hands of men and women. Possibly the right hand of a man shows the Cortex, the left shows the Medulla, while female hands are reversed. To get proof as to which part of a gland is at fault presents difficulties to a layman.

Hypothenar Eminence

Evidence for the correlation of the spleen with the mount of the percussion, Luna is circumstantial and again needs verification but is perhaps worthy of comment. Researchers at the International Institute for Psychic Investigation did a great deal of work to try to find out if and how mediums are affected physically when under trance and similar mediumistic conditions. The spleen was identified as showing definite alterations of size, weight, etc. On the hand as the psychic faculties are employed the lower half of the palm at the percussion becomes pink and yet more roseate, returning to the pale pink of the habitual sensitive hand when the demonstration is ending. Of course when a spleen is at fault the physical blood supply suffers, which makes the whole hand lack energy.

Hereditary Fault

There is another aspect of skin pattern marking to which I want to draw the attention of those people who look after backward and afflicted children. The hand looks to be covered with what can only be described as 'blotches', but the condition is difficult to describe until prints have been seen and noted. Enormous care must be taken that the hand is absolutely clean and free from perspiration when the prints are taken. But, when two prints have been taken and both show the same blotched pattern in exactly the same places, one can be nearly sure that the basic cause is, in Biblical terms, that the sins of the fathers are being visited upon the children even unto the third and fourth generation. My experience has not been sufficient to be beyond question, but among children at a mentally retarded school one found this blotching so often that I venture to wonder whether the suppression of V.D. in parent or grandparent may affect the matrix or inherent pattern which must inform the original cell how to divide itself into the marvellous design of a human mechanism. The condition appears on many prints shown by other workers among these poor young people, and we can say that in the very blotched hand of a backward or afflicted child one can suspect the after-effects of venereal diseases. I also feel that if the danger were more recognized public opinion might help many of the inherently clean young teenager type to be more fastidious.

Blotching may occur also as the result of other chronic

infections such as malaria (Fig. 100). In the pre-polio print white marks may be discerned inside the Life Line and across the lower part of the hand to the Hypothenar. The theory should be tested further that with infection the blotches may

Fig. 100—Typical blotching, probably malaria

appear at random while those caused by shock tend to be in and on lines.

T.B.

Traditionally Hippocrates has the credit of having observed the effect of a wasting tuberculosis on the Index finger, and his name is used for the condition when the disease is advanced and the finger clubs at the tip, turning inwards towards the palm.

Having watched my own nails rise from their beds when my heart was infected while my lungs remained in perfect order I cannot accept the theory of consumption or lung trouble. This view was supported by a colleague who nursed in a T.B. sanatorium and did not find one example. On the other hand, a medical Member of the S.S.P.P. has found the highly curving nail on a number of people suffering an infection of the bronchia and throat parts of the breathing apparatus. As my own nails grew out they returned to normal, so the trouble must have been a disturbance of the bed of the nail and not the root or matrix. This rising up must have come from the infection and blockage of the little ducts beneath the horn. I postulate that the true cause is a lack of oxygen, which is so necessary to make the various constituents work together thus causing blockages in the ducts and capillaries through lack of oxidization.

On recovery, while the hard sheath could not flatten again, the new part found no obstacles to surmount. *Lack of oxygen* as a cause would fit the affection of the bronchia and throat, while the T.B. patients in an open air sanatorium would have had such a surplus around them that enough could get through to the nails.

Nails often grow a ridge across during illness or injury which grows out in six to eight months. In general illness or fever the ridges may show on both hands though where only one side of the body has been concerned I have seen the ridges on the corresponding hand only.

To return to respiratory maladies—the danger area seems to begin a good deal further down the hand with a breakdown of the skin pattern within the Life Line, about level with the upper boundary of the thumb. The formation often takes the form of a barren looking whitish area interspersed with dots. The dot pattern sometimes accompanies the Life Line for half an inch or more, suggesting a period of time for the duration of the ill-health.

When the line of dots is quite narrow but accompanies the line for some distance Jaquin states that he has found catarrh. I have examples endorsing this view so that when formation is in or close to the line itself look for catarrh rather than tuberculosis, but the chronic catarrh should not be neglected.

The first effect is to make the line look untidy, as though it had not been engraved cleanly, always an indication that all is not well with whichever line has this appearance.

When the threat of danger to the lungs is established the disruption of the skin pattern may spread to the mount of the Index finger. I think that only in an advanced stage, when oxygen is seriously lacking, does the Hippocratic condition develop.

Throat

A clearly chained Life Line as it passes under the first finger registers a history of throat infection and bronchial trouble, especially in childhood. During our inquiry into signs of deafness we found chaining where deafness had resulted from such infection in childhood.

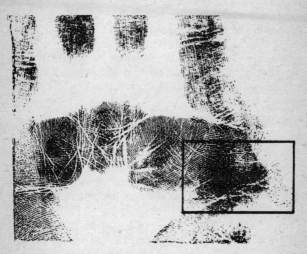

Fig. 101—Deafness from childhood throat infection

Deafness

The S.S.P.P. has not yet enough examples to be satisfied that we have established the signs on the hand, particularly since difficulties in hearing can arise from so many different causes. The traditional marking is a large island on the Heart Line under the Saturn finger. This island was present on some of our prints but by no means upon them all. Flexibility of the top joint of the Little finger seems an infallible guide to quickness of hearing, an ultra stiff one does not hear telephone bells and so on. For accuracy of hearing (Chapter IV, Part One) we went to the Mount of Venus and looked for height there. So far the findings in difficulties of hearing have been rather negative, perhaps they will be more defined in a later edition. Mrs. St. Hill found a row of white dots on the Head Line under the Medius finger in some (undefined) forms of deafness.

Sight

Eye complaints can show as a rather large, definite island on the Heart line under the third finger or, traditionally, cataract makes a small, clear circle on the thumb side of the Life Line, with a half circle for one eye only. This circle was quite definite on my mother's hands but we need evidence as to whether the mark remains after the operation.

I think that when the island appears on the Heart Line the cause should be sought in mineral imbalance. This will be discussed further in the next chapter.

Teeth

Just above the Heart Line between the third and fourth fingers, is the area in sympathy with teeth and gums. Little, fine lines, very delicately etched, is the usual demonstration but the ridging can break into a pattern of missing nerve endings on each separate ridge instead of a smooth line. Should the bacteria become stronger the pattern will break up more and more.

There is a part of the Mount of Venus which hollows when people pass about fifty years of age and I cannot assign any suitable gland to the position. Often the tendon which draws the thumb towards the middle finger shows an alignment when the hand is outstretched. From that tendon down the palm to an imaginary line from the lower joint of the thumb to the third finger seems to hollow thus extending the 'Plain of Mars'.

Reproductive organs

The true area of the *reproductive organs* is found at the base of the palm on the other, Hypothenar, side near the wrist.

Whether there is veiling, heavy lining, or a breakdown of skin pattern at the bottom corner of the Mount of Luna there should be a check of those organs as the source of malaise.

There is also support for Cheiro's statement that a sharp rise of the first racette into the palm is a warning of difficulty in childbirth. I have been told of a tented arch in the skin pattern, rising in the same place on to the Mount of Neptune, proving to be the same warning but I have not verified this myself.

To return to the mystery hollow, unless there is a good, nicely developed Thenar Eminence there is not enough life in the hand, and therefore the owner, to enjoy the warmth of human relationships; so the sinking of the upper part of the mount must picture the decrease of youthful fervour, of the blood coursing through the veins, including the palmar arches.

LINES

Life Line

The Life Line, in addition to the relationship with throat and respiratory organs at its commencement under the Index, is supposed to represent the Spinal Column as the course passes under the Medius. My own view is that the line is more closely allied with the nerves of the spine, rather than the vertebrae. I have seen diagrams of a very strong line indeed that suffered an injury in which some of the nerves were trapped, resulting in total paralysis from just below the shoulder blades downwards. With incredible courage the patient was kept alive for about a dozen years. The Life Line slowly broke up, ultimately fading out at the wrist end. The patient was able to use his hands which he did making models, writing, painting, etc., on the days when he felt well enough to do so, therefore it was not lack of use which made the line fade out.

I have also seen Life Lines of patients who have damaged vertebrae and shown minor signs, but not the dramatic break of the damaged nerve column. Once again it seems the nervous system to which the lines respond.

Mercury Line

Perhaps the most important and certainly the most debated of all the lines from the health angle is that which lies between the base of the hand and the mount beneath the Little finger. The old books name the line for the Liver and assign all alimentary troubles to its path. The basic common denominator, I suggest, is that the line represents our awareness of our autonomic nervous system. The longer the line runs the greater the degree of awareness until, as the line crosses the Heart Line, and ends on the mount beneath the Little finger, we respond all too quickly to emotional stimulus. We feel literally sick with emotions of unhappiness and recover from physical ailments when we are happy or determined.

Hands are frequently found completely without this line when the lucky owner is unaware that he has such a nervous system. He leaves his vagus and phrenic nerves to get on with their own work without interference.

Of course the line may break and start again, or show islands when illness is felt; but if the illness is regarded as a chance of a rest or a holiday no island or break need appear. The little dashes of line between breaks seem to report spasmodic occasions when the owner is aware of his absence of health and may coincide with illness, while an island may show a prolonged period of ill-health and anxiety about the cause.

I name this line, whatever the origin at the wrist end, the 'Headline of the sub-conscious' which is, I think, an accurate description. See also page 175.

Heart Line

The Heart or Upper Horizontal Line as it passes from the percussion under the fourth and third fingers shows the state of the blood passing through that organ. The question will be pursued further in Chapter V, Mineral Imbalance.

Head Line

The Head or Proximal Transverse Line is distorted in many of the mental disorders studied by Dr. Wolff. Apart from the cuts and dots we found in the psychological aspect the line is also subject to islands which may denote a period of anxiety, of illness in which the head is involved, but islands may also be due to potassium deficiency. A chain is more likely to be due to a deficiency cause whereas one island is more likely to be due to a definite pain or illness.

Poor Lines

Among groups of young people in their late teens or early twenties there are many hands showing indefinite and pale marking as though all were feeling overtaxed and uncertain. The lines look as undernourished and overtired as their owners probably are, especially when the young folk are working for examinations and cutting sleep short to get the social side in as well, the condition is very like the weariness of insomnia. The picture of the sleepless hand is difficult to portray in words but a study of Fig. 58, page 132 will show a shallow untidiness of line that always leads to questions about sufficient sleep and an appeal for at least one good night's sleep each week.

A Fellow of the S.S.P.P. when in hospital noticed that many of her comrades in the ward showed a diamond-shaped pattern between, or partly formed by, the lines of Life and Fate about one-quarter to one-third of the palm from the wrist. She has since observed many hands of people who have had internal operations and found that in all cases there has been some diamond-shaped device there. Hysterectomy invariably shows clearly but she had found a similar pattern after an operation to remove a gall-bladder.

The S.S.P.P. is continuing the investigation because only time will prove whether, when someone has the mark but has not had an internal operation, they are going to have one, or whether the findings have been coincidental. The removal of an appendix does not appear to be included as a serious internal operation.

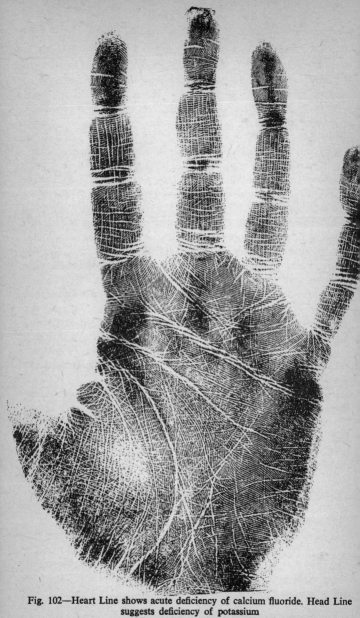

Fig. 102—Heart Line shows acute deficiency of calcium fluoride. Head Line suggests deficiency of potassium

CHAPTER V

MINERAL IMBALANCE AND
TWO WARNINGS

'GIVE US the tools and we will finish the job.' So said Sir Winston Churchill, when he set Britain to work in the Second World War. And so echo the cells of all animal bodies, including Man.

Fate has forced upon me the study of mineral imbalance both from a human and a veterinary angle so, with all the difficulties of testing both for basic and trace elements, I saw there might be easy and available clues on the hands. Again, the ever recurring chorus—there is so much more work to be done on the subject—but if I give my own short list it may inspire further seeking.

The following elements are examples of which I have had experience and suggest they are identified on the hand.

Calcium Fluorica	Molybdenum
Calcium Phosphate	Manganese
Copper (Cuprum)	(Iridium)
Iodine	(Osmium)
Tin (Stannum)	(Titanium)
Zinc	Silica
Potassium (Kali)	Iron (Ferrum)

Calcium Fluorica deficiency is shown by lines beneath the Heart Line under the third and fourth fingers. Sometimes there is a small ladder of three or four rungs leading up to the line; sometimes the ladder is not so pronounced, but where there is a doubling of the Heart Line without the ends closing in to form islands the answer will be calcarea fluorica deficiency. Calcium is essential building material for bones, arteries and veins, for teeth and hair, for the web-like covering of the brain inside the skull and all important tissues of animal bodies. The deficiency can cause insomnia.

Calcium Phosphate is especially useful to young bones, and to raising the tone of tired tissues, but it does not seem to make the same pattern on the hand. So far as I have been able to ascertain, it can only be identified by brittle nails and/ or white spots on the nails. These white spots are very prevalent in the New Forest where there is a marked deficiency of calcium for all animal life.

When I was farming there we had a truck-load of chalk from the railway which had to be brought three miles to the farm in a small trailer, necessitating many journeys. By dusk, and the last load, the field being treated had no less than seventeen of those most nervous animals, deer, who did not run away when we spread the load but turned the lumps of chalk over with their fore-hooves, greedily eating the grass beneath. A dark chestnut filly, from a Forest dam by a polo pony sire, had very bad eczema when she changed her coat if she did not have adequate 'churn flour' (the trade name for a useful form of calcium additive). She was sold locally with a cocoa tin of her coat-changing tonic. Her new mistress forgot to give it to her and the rash appeared along her underneath. Her 'doctor' was baffled and her mistress angry. Given the needed calcium the weeping rash had healed over by next morning with complete recovery in a few days.

Among human people who showed the 'ladder' beneath the Heart Line one can get an equally dramatic effect. One woman who had not slept naturally since the arrival of her third child, fell asleep for twelve hours after her first dose of Calcium Fluorica. A small boy, whose first teeth had degenerated and also could not sleep, had calcium (homeopathically prepared 30. Potency) six nights each week with iodine on Sundays. He then enjoyed undisturbed nights and grew a beautiful set of adult teeth of which his school dentist approved unreservedly term after term.

Iodine. Another fact was brought home most vividly. 'Churn' flour used to upgrade New Forest ponies and to grow coats on champion show poodles had one ounce of iodine to one hundredweight of meal. When we tried some without iodine results were so poor as to be useless. But they all recovered quickly when iodine was again used. In Kenya where there is no calcium in the soil people used to iodine intake from our surrounding sea, did not respond to calcium until iodine was added.

Copper deficiency shows in the fading of the lines. As the girl who caused my introduction to fading lines actually died as the lines in her right hand faded, I was especially anxious for and impressed by the second case. Cuprum, taken homeopathically, started the second woman's return to health and she was most intrigued to watch the rubbed out lines returning to normal. I have observed the same effect many times since and am sure that this fading out is of the utmost importance when people are overtired or 'off-colour.'

The commercial use of the mineral itself supports our theory that lines are formed by the action and response of nerves. Nerves transmit electrical impulses to perform their work. Copper is used extensively for conducting electricity in wires, etc. When the copper part of a wire is damaged no electricity flows. When copper is in short supply in the human frame the lines fade.

Furthermore copper deficiency often seems to be the cause of morning sickness in pregnancy; probably the infant is needing a good deal to start its own nervous system so mother supplies the requirement from her own vagus and phrenic nerves. With small doses, preferably in homeopathic triturated form for ease of assimilation, to feed the mother's own nerves, the sickness disappears in a couple of days.

Iron (Ferrum). The iron in a human body is said to be only enough for a six inch nail but without that nail the body falls to pieces. The appeal for more is shown by paleness of the lines of a hand. With copper at fault the lines look as though they had been rubbed out with an india-rubber; when iron is in short supply lines do not lose their form but lose colour, often with a smooth whitish band where the line should be when the palm is stretched out but showing a clear, pale line when the palm is relaxed. All animal life becomes tired, run-down, washed out in hair and skin when short of that X millionth particle of iron for the heart of the cells that need it.

Some people cannot absorb their iron even when taken in suitable vegetables while tonics make them sick. Some American tonics include a trace of *Molybdenum* which acts as a catalyst and makes the iron more easily absorbed.

Commercially molybdenum is mixed with iron at the second stage of the path to steel which, apart from other considerations, vastly increases the range of heat at which iron can be worked. Molybdenum has a very high degree of valency so that it can exchange molecules with the iron atoms and thereby break the iron up into an absorbable form. The Agricultural Department of the New South Wales Government has done wonders for the crops by spraying with merely ounces of molybdenum to the acre and some experiments were under consideration in Kenya where grass is anaemic while growing out of iron soil.

(I always picture 'Moly' as a Cockney girl swapping her befeathered hat with iron's bowler!)

Other trace elements are sometimes required to help in the absorption of iron as, for instance, *Manganese*. I am not happy about the signs on the hands which differentiate between the need for molybdenum or manganese to act as catalysts for iron, but I suggest that height above sea level may come into the picture. When people in Kenya took a short course of manganese, for about a fortnight, before going on their holiday to the coast they derived much more benefit much more quickly. This is only a query but, at the high levels, 5,000 to 8,000 feet of the uplands, Cosmic radiation is not very diffused; when a particle reaches sea level—according to the records of the Science Museum, London—its mesoms, electrons, etc., have spread over half a square mile. Life is responsive to Cosmic radiation and it is feasible that manganese comes into the picture of our reception and use through the Pineal Gland and Spleen.

These ideas are not universally accepted yet but there is enough evidence for more adventurous minds to investigate. If manganese does stimulate the spleen it *might* show by a reinforcement and clearing of skin pattern on the palmar side of the Hypothenar Eminence (see map) and the Mount of Neptune near the wrist.

Iridium. This valuable trace element has not yet been identified on hands but where an island on the Heart Line accompanies eye troubles and the gross building materials such as calcium, iron, potassium and silica are in adequate supply, the island may refer to the three essential trace elements for eyes, iridium, osmium and titanium. With osmium at fault look for the threat of a circle for cataract on the thumb side of the Life Line.

Radium. I have only one example of which the cause is certain. The tips of all the fingers crack open where the nail ends, the cracks are deep and painful and do not heal easily.

Tin (Stannum) affects the nervous system, with a tendency to drop things for no apparent reason. Overgrown cuticles to the nails may also show the lack of this trace element.

Potassium (Kali) shortage leads to a chaining of the Head Line and may be responsible for a similar type of continuous islands in other lines such as the Heart and Mercury Lines. Kali Phos (Schuessler) is not only one of the great nerve remedies showing in the disruption of lines, but it is also used for nose and throat troubles which find an echo in the islands at the early part of the Life Line we studied in the last chapter. (Fig. 102, page 238).

Silica. When the rheumatic warning of a veil appears on the percussion side of the hand between the two transverse lines showing trouble in the Suprarenal Glands think of silica. This, the twelfth Schuessler Salt is a great tidier but a very slow worker. Cysts, adhesions, over-abundance of calcium are all put in order by this remedy and I think the actual work is done by the improved and active Suprarenal Gland.

A pony I owned had terrible adhesions left after a severe operation, causing him much pain. Directly he came out of his stable on to granite setts his head went down and he licked and licked the granite. Powdered silica was put into his feed, in addition to other treatment, and in about three weeks he could stand on the setts without any temptation to tiresomeness. The treatment plus silica cured him completely and he lived a happy, useful life till he was twenty-one.

Zinc. According to South Australian Agricultural experiments zinc is essential to the growth of wheat. Their work in the 'desert' between South and Western Australia proved that after all the usual fertilizers had been duly tried a few pounds of zinc to the acre increased the yield twenty-fold.

This knowledge leads to the question whether the severe treatment of the grain for white bread and the removal of so much of the germ, is not responsible for the prevalence of ailments to the spine such as 'slipped disc', etc. This in turn led us to look for zinc deficiency in the Life Line and I found a few nice examples of very fine, narrow chaining starting where the line passes under the area of the Medius finger. In one clear case the age of onset happened to coincide, so whether the position in fact referred to age or to the Saturnian connection with the skeleton one cannot be sure. The S.S.P.P. is asking for more examples of faulty backs which do not arise from accidental injury.

TWO WARNINGS

I claim to have discovered two patterns in the lines of the hand which could be extremely useful when, if ever, they are recognized.

1.   A warning signal when someone has had a serious shock either emotional or physical.

When all three main lines of Heart, Head and Life unite beneath the first finger, even if the upper line does but send a branch, there is a certain indication of the danger of the effect of delayed shock. The emotion of the Heart Line does not escape through the fingers in dramatic relief, the owner seems quiet, calm, and apparently unaffected, and does the wise actions demanded; but three, four or five weeks later, according to the personal rhythm, strange illnesses appear which may manifest as one of the arthritis group, heart affection, and so on. The shock has been driven deep down into

Fig. 103—Lines together under Index

the depths of his or her being and will make its effect felt in its own time. In sum, do not trust a patient who appears none the worse if they have that formation on both hands but treat as for serious shock at the time with no nonsense about carrying on bravely; and suspect them if they have it on one hand only.

2. The other warning sign found on hands is a strong line or group of lines on the base of the percussion. This was also discovered by Spier and mentioned in detail in his book *The Hands of Children*, as the 'poison' line. Often this line goes right across the base of the palm between the two proximal mounts when it used to have the reputation of the name 'Via Lascivia'. I have seen a very poor, faded outline on the hands

of a recovered alcoholic but one often sees varieties of this line on the hands of people who are most abstemious in every way. Spier says of it—'People who have it feel an instinctive aversion to all kinds of poisons, such as allopathic medicaments, alcohol, etc., and at the same time are very sensitive to the effect of these and other poisons.'

Fig. 104—Poison Line. See also Fig. 83 (Via Lascivia) page 178

I have found that people react in different ways but never do they react as expected. Sometimes, for instance, they tell you with pride that 'It took enough anaesthetic for a horse' before their operation, but usually they respond too quickly. It might be that had the 'horse' ones been tried with a minimum dose they would not have reacted so strongly—but when the line across the Hypothenar Eminence is strong it is as a road sign—proceed carefully, road unsafe.

The hand seems to respond to Nature in that Mount of the Moon, racial memories, early memories, feeling for the rhythm of the seasons, weather, and even dancing leaves. So, when we remember that all lines show our awareness of the forces in sympathy with the part of the hand on which they appear, it is logical that a line there should show an extra awareness for and kinship with the more natural fruits of the earth.

APPENDIX AND BIBLIOGRAPHY

ARISTOTLE, (384–322 B.C.) is reputed to be the first of the Western writers on hands, having recorded the knowledge he gained in Egypt at the behest of Alexander the Great.

ARPENTIGNY, C. S. le Comte d' (1798–1865) Officer in the Army of Napoleon. On his retirement he noticed that the engineer friends who visited a neighbour had hands of a very different shape from the hands of the artists, poets and intelligentsia who frequented the salon of the lady of the house. D'Arpentigny continued his observations to found the art of Chirognomy.

BASHIR, Mir B.A. came to England in 1947, joined the S.S.P.P. to become Chairman in 1952 and 1953. *How to Read Hands* (Thorsons Publishers Limited) is his only publication to date but his many lessons and lectures have been of great value. Perhaps his most outstanding contributions have been his insistence on the true boundaries of the palm and his evaluation of the skin pattern apex on the Mount of Jupiter; but each of his talks to the Society have given some gem to test and include in one's chirological vocabulary.

BENHAM, Dr. William G. first published his *Laws of Scientific Palmistry* in December 1900 (Knickerbocker Press, New York). Dr. Benham recounts how he first became interested in hands at the age of thirteen. He took up a career in Medicine in order to study the effect of health on hands and also studied the hands of eminent men in different walks of life that he might advise young people about their vocations. Dr. Benham founded the Institute of Vocational Guidance in New York and continued his interest in the work until his death at well over eighty years of age.

BAINES, Arthur E. was editor of *The Electrical Engineer* when, in May 1885 he published an article entitled The Human Body as a Disturbing Element in Electrical Testing. Chance led him to discover electrical response in fruit and his *Studies in Electrical Physiology* (Animal and Vegetable) (George Routledge & Sons Ltd. 1918) laid the foundations for the study of the electrical impulses activating nerves.

CHEIRO. The last and greatest of pre-1914 Palmists. Most of the subsequent books are based on his teachings. *The Language of the Hand* or *You and Your Hand* sum up his philosophy of hand interpretation. The author met Cheiro in 1912 and is ever appreciative of his kindness to a very ordinary client. The great man took time to give what was virtually a lesson while considering what to say about a hand he saw was doomed. A most valuable part of the lesson lay in the demonstration of the care he took in the interpretation and disclosure of what one thinks one sees in a hand though, with Cheiro, the judgement was supported by Astrology, Numerology and by his personal gift of seership.

CHIROLOGICAL SOCIETY. Founded in April 1889 with Mrs. Katherine St. Hill (q.v.) as President. Under her guidance the Members followed a systematic search for truth in hand interpretation. They visited hospitals, prisons, mental homes and to their observation is due the relation between the nerves in the brain and the lines on the hand. This aspect was not acknowledged by the Medical and Anthropological worlds for a long time but has, by 1960, gained acceptance. The Society faded out during the 1939–45 war.

COMPTON, Miss Vera. Pupil and successor of Noel Jaquin (q.v.) *Palmistry for Everyman* (Everyman's Library). Articles on the similarities and differences of the hands of twins, triplets and other multiple births may be found in the back numbers of *Prediction*.

CUMMINS, Dr. Harold Ph.D. Professor of Microscopic Anatomy, Tulane University of Medicine. *Finger Prints, Palms and*

Soles (The Blakiston Company, Philadelphia 1943) was written in collaboration with his Associate Professor of Microscopic Anatomy, Dr. Charles Midlo, M.D. In the Preface Dr. Cummins pays tribute to Harris H. Wilder and his wife Inez, who introduced him to the study of Dermatoglyphics. The book has much historical and statistical interest for the serious student.

DEBRUNNER, Dr. Hugo. Swiss Psychologist. In 1941 he used handprints in conjunction with the Swiss Army and made experimental tests orientated on Körper—'the psychology of gesture'. He compared these systematically with handwriting, spontaneous drawings (doodles) and face and body structures; also with dreams and creative expressions. The results have been constantly and statistically evaluated.

Since 1950 he has extended his diagnostic researches on hand and foot structures on all ages right down to pre-natal development, in addition he examined members of various races and cultures and extended his studies to primates. The biological and anthropological researches incorporated also all the aspects of the papillary lines.

His collection consists of numerous hand and foot prints, among them more than 400 prints of apes. Dr. Debrunner showed me many examples from his files, was so generous-minded as to take an interest in the indications of personality we had formulated and I owe a great deal to his guidance. His many short, published articles have not yet been properly translated from the German.

DESBARROLLES, A. A. (1801–1886) A French artist, exiled to Spain during a revolution, lived and painted among the Gypsies and persuaded them to reveal some of their lore. When he returned to France he devoted his life to establishing the truth about Chirology. His work with the complementary work of d'Arpentigny, was translated into English by E. Heron Allen in the *Science of the Hand* and his *Manual of Chirosophy*.

FAULDS, Dr. Henry (1843–1930) was a Scottish Medical Missionary in Japan when he noticed finger prints on pre-history pottery which seemed to be a form of signature. He looked upon the prints as of anthropological value and wrote about them to Sir Charles Darwin who sent the letter on to his cousin Mr. (later Sir Francis) Galton. Two years later, in 1880, Dr. Faulds wrote to *Nature* suggesting that such prints might be a means of identification. His theory was confirmed by Sir William Herschel, Commissioner of Police in India, who had seen finger prints used on receipts for pensions etc. E. R. Henry published his classification of finger prints for purposes of identification in 1900. This scheme was adopted by Scotland Yard and is still the most widely used system. By 1911 Sir William, Dr. Faulds, Sir Francis Galton and Henry had persuaded the Police to take up the method seriously.

GALTON, Sir Francis (1822–1911) had followed up the suggestion that digital patterns might be of genetic and diagnostic value. He pioneered in basic studies on finger prints, including classification, inheritance and racial variations. The classification he organized into loops, whorls and arches and collected many thousands of specimens of finger prints. He was able to prove, by means of repeated printings of individuals after long periods, that the pattern does not alter, though it enlarges with normal growth and the texture may fail, but the pattern retains its form. At his death the collection passed to University College, London, where he endowed a professorship in Eugenics.

From *New Scientist*, 8, 129, 14th July 1960. (L. S. Penrose, M.D., F.R.S.)

Human Genetics

In his old age, Galton became concerned with the problem of improving the human stock, which he termed 'Eugenics', and he started an organization for assembling data, called the Eugenics Record Office, in Gower Street in 1904. The University of London eventually recognized the Francis Galton Laboratory officially in 1933. It was under the directorship of R. A. Fisher until 1945. From the first, the notion of Eugenics was interpreted very widely and the Laboratory has become concerned entirely with collecting facts about heredity, almost exclusively about human heredity, and with their scientific interpretation. It is in no way concerned with eugenical propaganda. There is a small permanent academic staff and a less permanent population of research assistants, postgraduate students and visiting scientists. Many of the results of these researches are published in detail in the *Annals of Human Genetics*, formerly *Annals of Eugenics*.

GALTON LABORATORY. From: *History of the College* (in U.C.L. Calendar)

In the allied field of statistics and eugenics a separate Department of Applied Statistics was created in 1911, and the Galton Chair of Eugenics was instituted.

(Karl Pearson was the first Galton Professor.)

During the time Professor Karl Pearson was Galton Professor, Dr. Ethel M. Elderton made some studies on the inheritance of finger prints collected from families. No further work was done in the Galton Laboratory on dermatoglyphics until Professor L. S. Penrose became Galton Professor in October 1945. He had become interested in the subject when Medical Officer for Ontario, when, just before his appointment to the Galton Chair of Eugenics, Professor Norma Ford Walker of Toronto drew his attention to Professor Cummins' (Tulane University, New Orleans, Louisiana) findings concerning the palm-prints of mongolian imbeciles and to the possibilities of dermatoglyphics.

Towards the end of 1945 collections of palm- and finger-prints were begun for the study of the genetics of metrical characters. These consisted of the prints of a representative but unrelated sample of the English population together with those of families (parents and children and sibs, including twins). At the same time a collection of finger- and palm-prints of mongols and their parents and brothers and sisters was begun. Dermal prints of inherited abnormalities of the hands and feet (such as lobster-claw and polydactyly) were also collected and analysed.

Later, in 1959, after it had been shown that mongolism was due to chromosomal abnormality, the study of the finger-, palm- and sole-prints of persons with other aberrant chromosomes was begun, including comparisons with normal controls.

(The information about Sir Francis Galton and the Galton Laboratory was graciously contributed by Dr. Sarah B. Holt, Ph.D. of the Galton Laboratory.)

JAQUIN. To Noel Jaquin we are indebted for much valuable pioneer work on the psychological attitude to life as shown by finger-print patterns, and for his observations on the disruption of the orderly sequence in ridge pattern as a warning of breakdown in constitution threatening organic disease. Mr. Jaquin has written many books of which *The Hand of Man* (Faber, 1934), *The Hand Speaks* (Lyndoe & Fisher Ltd. 1942), *Signature of Time* (Faber and Faber, 1950) *The Human Hand, The Living Symbol* (Rockcliff, 1956) are perhaps, the most helpful.

MANGIN, Henri., A French Chirologist who was in close touch with the Medical profession, several of his collaborators writing forewords to his books. He became interested in hands in 1929 and began publishing articles in *Hippocrate*, March and April 1939. *Telle Main Tel Homme* (1946), *La Main, Portrait De L'Homme* (1947), *Abrégé De Chiroscopie Médicale* (1950) gathered up many of his articles into book form while *Valeur Clinique Des Ongles* explains in detail his thoughts about nails. There have been several editions, Joseph-Charles, Griffon d'Or and Dangles, all of Paris, are responsible for the S.S.P.P. library copies.

PURKENJE. (1787–1869.) Dr. Jan Evangelista Purkenje is the originator of the scientific approach to skin pattern or dermatoglyphics. A brilliant Czech doctor and scientist, he was appointed to a professorship at Breslau in 1823 where, to justify his position with his German colleagues, he published a treatise on the work he had been doing at Prague on eye and hand.

To Dr. Purkenje we owe the observation of the spiral sweat glands in the skin, the patterns made by their alignment, the classification of those patterns and his conjectures about their genetic and diagnostic importance. His work has been translated by Henry J. John M.D. (American Philosophical Society, Independence Square, Philadelphia). The frontispiece portrait by Zd. Burian, Prague (reproduced by courtesy of Pastnickova, Prague) shows the Doctor as a very good-looking man with deep-set, dark eyes. In a later picture the artist has painted his hands with high hypothenar and finger mounts, long fingers, especially Mercury, and the right hand shows a sharp angle of sound which suggests the accuracy of the picture since he won his education by singing in the choir of the Piarist Order.

SAINT-GERMAIN, Comte C. de, A.B., L.L.M. of the University of France *The Study of Palmistry for Professional Purposes* (T. Werner Laurie Limited 1934) is a complete reference book on the life and work of Desbarrolles and d'Arpentigny. Originally published in Chicago in 1897–98 it constitutes a dictionary and book of reference to the beginning of modern Chirology.

ST. HILL, Mrs. Katharine Ashton, founded the Chirological Society in April 1889, and edited the journal *The Palmist's Review* for some years. *The Book of the Hand* (1927), *Medical Palmistry, Hands and Faces* (all Rider and Co.) and my own first guidance her *Grammar of Palmistry* are the result of the findings of the Society on the subject. Mrs. St. Hill shared with Dr. Purkenje an abhorrence of accepting old book lore without observing for herself, and checking with an open mind, looking only for truth.

SEN, K. C. His *Hast Samudrika Shastra* or *The Science of Hand Reading Simplified* (D. B. Taraporevala Sons & Co: Bombay) explains the connections between Eastern and Western interpretations and is enlightening to a student of pure palmistry.

SOCIETY FOR THE STUDY OF PHYSIOLOGICAL PATTERNS was founded by Noel Jaquin on 12th April 1945. The objects were defined as:

(a). To further the study of and research into the meaning and value of the Physiological Pattern as diagnostic evidence in psychological and pathological connections.

(b). To prove and stabilize the scientific importance of those studies.

The course of activities includes one lecture each month, a Group to analyse hypotheses, traditional interpretations, etc., classes for beginners, a library of relevant books, an extensive filing system of vocations, disease and dermatoglyphic patterns where they suggest gifts or potentialities.

There is also a Journal in which are recorded the activities of the Society.

SPIER. Julius Spier died during the 1939–1945 war leaving his intended trilogy unfinished. Only *The Hands of Children* was completed, though a second edition, with an appendix by Hester R. Levi, included the notes Spier had made towards his intended *Hands of the Mentally Diseased* (Routledge & Kegan Paul, 1955). Spier's lectures at Zurich University converted Dr. C. G. Jung to the study of hands. Many former pupils follow his work.

WOLFF, Dr. Charlotte, was one of the people who owe much to Spier. Her *Studies in Hand Reading* translated from the German (1936) was followed by *The Human Hand, The Hand in Psychological Diagnosis* and *A Psychology of Gesture* (Methuen & Co. 1951).

WOOD JONES, Dr. F., D.Sc., F.R.S., F.R.C.S. was Professor of Anatomy at Manchester University when he wrote *The Principles of Anatomy as Seen in the Hand* (Baillière, Tindall and Cassell, Second edition 1946) from which the anatomical part of this book is so gratefully quoted.